PENTLAND FIRTH
To Orkney Islands
Scrabster
Thurso
Hoy Halt
Halkirk
Bower
Watten
Georgemas Junction
Bilbster
Wick
Scotscalder
Altnabreac
Forsinard
Lybster
Kinbrace
Borrobol Halt
Kildonan
Salzcraggie Halt
Helmsdale
Loth
Brora
The Mound
Dunrobin Halt (Private)
Golspie
Embo
Dornoch
Dornoch Firth
Tain
Fearn
Nigg
MORAY FIRTH
Fort George
Nairn
Forres
Kinloss
Brodie
Auldearn
Gollanfield
Dalcross
Allanfearn
Culloden Moor
Daviot
Moy
Dunphail
Dava
Grantown-on-Spey (West)
Broomhill
Carr Bridge
Aviemore
Kincraig
Kingussie
Newtonmore
Lossiemouth
Elgin
Alves
Calcots
Urquhart
Garmouth
Spey Bay
Portgordon
Portessie
Findochty
Portknockie
Cullen
Portsoy
Ladysbridge
Banff
Macduff
Buckie
Buckpool
Tillynaught
Cornhill
Glenbarry
Bridgefoot Halt
Ordens Halt
Golf Club House Halt
Lhanbryde
Orbliston
Longmorn
Orton
Mulben
Keith Junction
Knock
Rothes
Dandaleith
Craigellachie
Grange
Cairnie Junction
Rothiemay
Keith Town
Auchindachy
Towiemore
Drummuir
Huntly
Dufftown
Knockando
Blacksboat
Ballindalloch
Advie
Carron
Aberlour
Dailuaine Halt
Cromdale
Grantown-on-Spey (East)
Nethy Bridge
Boat of Garten Junction
Gartly
Kennethmont
Wardhouse
Insch
Oyne
Pitcaple
Inverurie
Kintore
Kinaldie
Pitmedden
Kittybrewster
Dyce
ABERDEEN
Fraserburgh
Kirkton Bridge Halt
Cairnbulg
St. Combs
Philorth Halt
Philorth Bridge Halt
Rathen
Lonmay
Strichen
Mormond Halt
Brucklay
Maud Junction
Auchnagatt
Mintlaw
Longside
Newseat Halt
Inverugie
Peterhead
Arnage
Ellon
Logierieve
Udny
Newmachar
To Orkney and Shetland Islands
Lumphanan
Torphins
Dess
Glassel
Aboyne
Dinnet
Cambus o' May Halt
Ballater
Banchory
Crathes
Park
Culter
Cults
STONEHAVEN
Inverbervie
Laurencekirk
Edzell
Brechin
MONTROSE
Bridge of Dun
Kirriemuir
FORFAR
Alyth
Alyth Junction
Blairgowrie
Coupar Angus
DUNDEE
West Ferry
Monifieth
Elliot Junction
ARBROATH
Easthaven
Carnoustie
Barry Links
Blair Atholl
Struan
Killiecrankie
Pitlochry
Balnaguard
Grandtully
Ballinluig
Aberfeldy
Guay
Dalguise
Dunkeld and Birnam
Murthly
SHETLAND ISLANDS
Foula
Lerwick
Fair I.
ORKNEY ISLANDS
Mainland
Stromness
Kirkwall
Pentland Firth
To Aberdeen

FRONT COVER PICTURES

Top Picture:
Unidentified Park Royal 4-wheel diesel railbus waits at the impressive former Caledonian Railway station at Crieff before taking the last service of the day to Comrie in June 1964.

Roy M.B. Crombie/SRPS

Bottom Picture:
EE Type 1 Bo-Bo D.E. #D8030 passes Throsk signal box at the south end of Alloa swing bridge with a train of power station coal from the Fife coalfield to Clydesmill power station on 14th September 1962.

John M. Boyes – The Armstrong Railway Photographic Trust

B.R. DIESEL TRACTION IN SCOTLAND

George C. O'Hara

Copyright:

First Published 2010
ISBN 978-0-9530821-2-4

Published by:

CLYARD NOVELLA LIMITED

Clyard Novella Limited
16 Garryhorn
PRESTWICK
South Ayrshire
Scotland KA9 2HU

Typesetting by:

Highlight

Highlight Type Bureau Ltd
4 Mornington Villas
Bradford
West Yorkshire BD8 7HB

Colour separation and reproduction by:

The Amadeus Press

The Amadeus Press
Ezra House
West 26 Business Park
Cleckheaton
West Yorkshire BD19 4TQ

Printed by:

The Amadeus Press

The Amadeus Press
Ezra House
West 26 Business Park
Cleckheaton
West Yorkshire BD19 4TQ

Bound by:

HUNTER HF FOULIS

Hunter & Foulis
Haddington,
East Lothian
Scotland EH41 3ST

Jacket design from an original sketch by E.M. O'Hara. circa 1986.

B.R. DIESEL TRACTION IN SCOTLAND

Contents

ACKNOWLEDGEMENTS

This book is a compilation of hundreds of pictures taken by about 30 of the most avid and artistic photographers of the operations, infrastructure and real estate of the former Scottish Region of British Railways. The spread of pictures depicted in this book was taken around the inception of dieselisation in the mid-1950's, until the privatisation of the industry in 1993.

The author has had the pleasure of knowing about these gentlemen, and later meeting most of them. He then became inspired by the creativity of some of their compositions. This enthusiasm to pursue railway photography was further spurred by the muted advocacy of the incessant contraction of much of the passenger route mileage, coupled with the virtual annihilation of all of the traditional freight network, which British Railways had inherited from the LMSR and LNER systems at the nationalisation of the railways in Britain in 1947.

As these esteemed railway photographers embraced old age, and their former profusion of photo-shoots diminished, they still remained yoked to their life-long interest in trains. This fact was irrefutably evident in their respective insistence that each priceless collection of railway negatives was safely acquired by either a bona fide preservation society or honourable committed individual who would painstakingly treasure their photographic material, and at the same time allow access by authors and publishers who sought rights of reproduction.

The author personally thanks the following individuals, their descendants, associations or societies for their assistance and permission to compile, edit and produce the spread of photographs set forth in this book.

J.M. Boyes (courtesy Richard Barber, Secretary of the Armstrong Railway Photographic Trust); Alan Carlaw; Roy M.B. Crombie/SRPS; David Cross (for permission to publish photos taken by his father Derek Cross); Mike Cooper; Ken Falconer; J.N. Faulkner; Max Fowler; John Spencer Gilks; Roy Hamilton (courtesy of Douglas Norris and the Strathspey Railway archives); Douglas Hume; Keith G. Jones; Jack Kernahan; J.M. McIntosh; Michael Mensing; Morrison Bryce; Robin Nelson; Tom H. Noble; Ken Nuttall; Geo. C. O'Hara; W.S. Sellar; Sandy Smeaton; David C. Smith; Hamish Stevenson; G.N. Turnbull; and Barry Hoper of The Transport Treasury (for permission to access, and reproduce part of the photographic collections of Norris Forrest, Sandy Murdoch and W.A.C. Smith).

The author is indebted for the input, effort and painstaking attention to detail by Hamish Stevenson/SRPS, with his review of the pictorial and narrative contents of this book. His comments and contributions of supplementary details have greatly increased the factual narrative of this book.

FOOTNOTE:
The publisher would like to contemplate companion volumes to this book. Any readers who know of railway photographic collections in their family or among friends or relatives are encouraged to contact either Clyard Novella Ltd. or The Transport Treasury, Logie Shannoch, Drumrossie, INSCH, Aberdeenshire, AB52 6LJ

SELECTIVE LIST OF ABBREVIATIONS USED IN THIS BOOK:

BRCW	Birmingham Railway Carriage & Wagon Co. Ltd.
BR	British Railways (usually workshops)
BSC	British Steel Corporation
BACo.Ltd.	British Aluminium Co. Ltd.
GLOUCESTER R.C.& W. CO. LTD.	Gloucester Railway Carriage & Wagon Co. Ltd.
NBL	North British Locomotive Co. Ltd.
LMSR	London Midland and Scottish Railway Co. Ltd.
LNER	London North Eastern Railway Co. Ltd
EE	English Electric
GSWR	Glasgow and South Western Railway
GNSR	Great North of Scotland Railway
HR	Highland Railway

INTRODUCTION

Diesel traction was introduced to the former Scottish Region of British Railways in the 1950's. It had come in the form of trial runs of DMU's which were built in England, and the allocation of diesel hydraulic and diesel mechanical shunting locomotives manufactured by the indigenous Scottish companies: The North British Locomotive Co. Ltd. and Andrew Barclay Sons & Coy Ltd. of Glasgow and Kilmarnock respectively. The more powerful and ultimately very reliable 350HP diesel electric shunters built in various BR workshops in England at the same time, and later known as class 08 were to prove to be one of the most enduring designs of diesel traction on the entire former BR network. Many examples were re-shopped, refitted and re-liveried throughout their lifetime.

The modernisation plan by the British Railways Board in 1955 was an overdue yet conversely bold and premature attempt at the replacement of steam engines by a range of drawing board designs of various types of diesel traction. The spectrum of locomotive and multiple unit types necessary to deliver this transformation was diverse. Designs were structured to produce anticipated tractive efforts and rigorous duty cycles which the credo of a modernisation railway system demanded. Generically this translated into the following categories of power classification for locomotives, irrespective of the types of transmission, viz:

Shunters up to 350HP		
Type 1 diesels above	350 HP	up to 999 HP
Type 2 diesels above	1000 HP	up to 1499HP
Type 3 diesels above	1500 HP	up to 1999HP
Type 4 diesels over	2000 HP	up to 2999HP
Type 5 diesels over	3000 HP	

Transmission types varied from diesel mechanical to diesel electric and diesel hydraulic.
Diesel multiple units were not unsurprisingly conceived and designed around the adaptation of existing types of proven bus engines with modified gearbox and transmission systems designed to accelerate and sustain the speeds that the multiple unit concept entailed.

The haste, versatility and commitment with which private locomotive and BR workshops adapted to the volume production of these new types of traction was formidable. Unfortunately several types were either not robust enough in design concept, or so poorly assembled, tested and accepted that the transition period from steam to diesel replacement lasted for effectively a decade. During this time the Scottish Region network contracted by about 30% of the track mileage total inherited by British Railways in 1948. This was a direct result of the "Reshaping of British Railways" or The Beeching Report which when published in 1963 rapidly led to the enactment to contract the entire UK railway network and also advocated the abandonment of many types of traditional railborne freight and the modus operandi by which this traffic was carried. Thus the character of traditional railway operations was about to be transformed by the replacement of the type of motive power used since the inception of the industry. In parallel with this development was the implementation of thorough and cheesepairing cost-benefit analysis of each and every line's raison d'être, the consequences of which pruned both route mileage, and all types of traffic carried throughout the entire Scottish Region.

Notwithstanding this dichotomy of investment in new types of traction, along with contraction of much of the network, the railway industry reluctantly cooperated with the plethora of government diktats and transport act amendments which emanated throughout this transition period. Lines closed with depressing regularity and freight traffic withered with each annual increase in the sizes of new lorries. Yet the hybrid fleet of new traction which exhibited varying degrees of reliability was made to work by a dedicated band of managers, engineering staff, locomotive, track, maintenance and signalling crews in an era of transient transport uncertainty.

In the period of four decades from the introduction of diesel traction until the government-enforced debacle that became UK railway privatisation, several types of locomotives and multiple units became synonymous with BR Scottish Region. All later endured the ignominy of drab corporate resprays, and the advent of TOPS computer identities in the form of five digit class identification in place of the previous 'D' or SC number prefix recognition.

This photographic album attempts to illustrate members of each class of locomotive and every type of diesel multiple units and diesel railbuses which worked on the former BR Scottish Region, along with routes where these trains operated. Selective chapters also depict engine sheds, goods yards, junctions, stations, marshalling yards and the diverse and unique types of traffic carried during this period by the railways of Scotland. The book appreciates the efforts, dedication and sheer professionalism displayed by all of the former employees of BR Scottish Region, who implemented constant changes to working practices against the background of an industry which was sometimes treated like an unwanted train-set by the hapless indifference, inconsistent transport policies and myopic dogma of each and every government during the existence of BR Scottish Region.

This book could not have been compiled and produced without the efforts and artistry of the many photographers who had the interest, vision and profound passion for the railways of Scotland during an era when the perceived romance of the steam age was being replaced by the soulless incursion of growling green boxes on bogies. Their visionary efforts to record this changing scene and the tacit cooperation of the management and employees of the former BR Scottish Region in allowing these photographs to be taken, is gratefully appreciated, and is manifested in the large and varied spectrum of railway scenes throughout Scotland from the mid-1950's until 1993. None of the photographs depicted can be replicated now or in the future. Types of traction, rolling stock, signals and track alignments, have all changed so significantly, that only major station buildings, tunnels and bridges remain from the era when the first generation of diesels came to work in Scotland.

The nomenclature used for locomotive and multiple unit identification, is as per that depicted when the type of traction was introduced. This means that the description of builders identity, initial power, wheel and transmission configuration and initial D prefix later becomes replaced by the respective TOPS five digit class identification numbers.

The photographs depicted in each section of this book have been arranged from the North to the South of Scotland, with the following exceptions: Section #1 (Engine Sheds), where the former British Railways numerical-alpha system of engine shed identification has been used. Section #2 (Diesel Railbuses), where the photographs have been set out from the West to the East of Scotland in a clockwise direction.

George C. O'Hara
Garryhorn,
PRESTWICK,
South Ayrshire
SCOTLAND
KA9 2HU

August 2010

Section 1

LOCO SHEDS & STABLING POINTS

At the inception of BR in 1948, there were 54 loco sheds, and a much lesser number of stabling points throughout the Scottish Region. All of these locations had been inherited from LMSR & LNER and had been provided to store, service, fuel and crew the entire fleet of steam locomotives in Scotland. These facilities were also called upon to provide ad-hoc coaling and water for visiting traction from the North of England.

With the gradual introduction of diesel locomotives, diesel multiple units and diesel railbuses onto the network, these existing sheds became the operational bases for these new forms of traction until new custom built facilities were built. Initially these existing sheds adopted the functional adjustments necessary to support the two different forms of traction. This hybridity of facilities was far from satisfactory, but was nevertheless necessary until the maintenance and servicing of steam locomotives was eradicated from Scotland in 1967.

The collection of photographs in this section illustrate several scenes of activity at some of these motive power depots, and latterly stabling points where locos were parked overnight, and the crews signed on at the start of each new shift. This spread of illustrations of operational traction at 30 former BR Scottish sheds and stabling points is laid out in the ascending numerical identity coding system which was part of the traction depot nomenclature of British Railways, i.e. from 60A to 68C.

LIST OF ENGINE SHEDS & STABLING POINTS ILLUSTRATED

1 INVERNESS (60A)
2 INVERNESS (60A)
3 AVIEMORE (60B)
4 FORRES (60E)
5 KITTYBREWSTER (61A)
6 FRASERBURGH
7 FRASERBURGH
8 FERRYHILL (61B)
9 FERRYHILL (61B)
10 KEITH (61C)
11 ELGIN
12 THORNTON JUNCTION (62A)
13 DUNDEE TAY BRIDGE (62B)
14 PERTH (63A)
15 ABERFELDY
16 ALLOA
17 OBAN (63E)
18 OBAN (63E)
19 ST. MARGARETS (64A)
20 LEITH CENTRAL
21 LEITH CENTRAL
22 EASTFIELD (65A)
23 PARKHEAD (65C)
24 DAWSHOLM (65D)
25 KIPPS (65E)
26 POLMADIE (66A)
27 SHIELDHALL
28 MOTHERWELL (66B)
29 LADYBURN (66D)
30 CORKERHILL (67A)
31 HURLFORD (67B)
32 AYR (67C)
33 AYR KYLE STREET (67C)
34 AYR (67C)
35 ARDROSSAN (67D)
36 STRANRAER (68C)

#1 Panoramic view of INVERNESS (60A) loco shed and carriage sheds on a snowy 4th April, 1968. Visible in this scene crammed with railway vehicles are four BRCW type 2 Bo-Bo D.E. and one BR 0-6-0 350 h.p. D.E. Shunter. *Douglas Hume*

#2 Stabled outside INVERNESS (60A) loco shed, and in front of the station is rail blue liveried Gloucester R.C. and W. Co. diesel railcar #SC55013 during August, 1970. This unit was regularly used to strengthen the BR Swindon 3-car DMU services between Inverness and Aberdeen for over two decades. *Geo. C. O'Hara*

#3 Stabled outside AVIEMORE (60B) loco shed in between working over the former HR main line via Grantown-on-Spey (West) and Dava, is an unidentified BRCW Type 2 Bo-Bo D.E. on a sunny June day in 1965, a few months before withdrawal of the passenger railway service on the line. *Roy M.B. Crombie/SRPS*

#4 BR 0-6-0 350 h.p. D.E. shunter #D3735 in quite clean external condition is seen just outside the former FORRES (60E) loco shed on 17th April, 1960. This locomotive was the last engine allocated to this shed. *Douglas Hume*

#5 NBL type 2 Bo-Bo D.E. #D6151 looking in ex-works condition is seen at the back of KITTYBREWSTER (61A) loco shed on 22nd June, 1960. Compare this view with photograph #697 taken over one decade later. *Ken Nuttall*

#6 Unidentified NBL Type 2 Bo-Bo D.E. comes off FRASERBURGH (sub-shed to Kittybrewster) on a very wet day in August, 1962, by which time all of the passenger and freight services on the Buchan Line had been dieselised.
Roy M.B. Crombie/SRPS

#7 BRCW Type 2 Bo-Bo D.E. #D5315 at FRASERBURGH (sub-shed of Kittybrewster) on 21st July, 1964, by which time the shed had closed, but was still in use as a stabling point. *Hamish Stevenson*

#8 The refuelling bay at FERRYHILL (61B) shed sees unidentified Brush Type 4 Co-Co, EE Type 1 Bo-Bo, and BRCW Type 2 Bo-Bo D.E. traction circa 1980. *Sandy Murdoch/TTT*

#9 EE Deltic Type 5 Co-Co D.E. #55015 "Tulyar" shares the refuelling bay at FERRYHILL (61B) shed with EE Type 4 1 Co-Co- D.E. #40125 during June, 1981. *Sandy Murdoch/TTT*

#10 Following the closure of KEITH (61C) shed at the advent of dieselisation on the lines between Inverness and Aberdeen, the location was still used as a stabling point for diesel locomotives working the yard, and the rump of the line to Dufftown. On 28th June, 1977, BR Type 2 Bo-Bo D.E. #25301 is stabled between duties with its engines running. Note the rakes of four wheel goods vans and wagons in the adjacent sidings. *Geo. C. O'Hara*

#11 Seen to good effect on 28th August, 1959, are the turntable, water tower and loco-coaling hoist of ELGIN (sub-shed of Keith) 61C. On shed are Ex-LNER K2. 2-6-0 #61782 leaking steam, with Andrew Barclay 0-4-0 205 h.p. D.M. shunter #D2414 seen in the background.
WAC Smith/TTT

#12 THORNTO JUNCTION (62A) loc shed on 20th August, 196 sees an unidentifie Clayton Type 1 Bo-Bo D. and a Metro-Camme DMU sharing the scen with several types c still functioning stea locomotives.
Douglas Hum

#13 Seemingly dumpe at the outside c DUNDEE TAY BRIDG (62B) shed sometime i the late 1960's are 3 NB 0-4-0 225 h.p. D.I shunters #'s D271 D2710 and D2713.
Sandy Murdoch/TT

#14 The refuelling bay at PERTH (63A) shed in July, 1965 sees three different classes of Type 2 Bo-Bo D.E.s all constructed by different locomotive builders. They are from left to right NBL (#D6119), BRCW (D5321) and BR (D5119) probably coupled together as a group for a top-up of their respective fuel tanks.

Sandy Murdoch/TTT

#15 The dilapidated former single road loco shed at ABERFELDY (sub shed of Perth 63A) forms the backdrop to BRCW Type 2 Bo-Bo D.E. #D5336 replenishing its train steam heating boiler from the still functional water column during January, 1965. Note brake composite coach #SC80417E. This vehicle later became operational on the SRPS Railway between Bo'ness and Kinneil.

Norris Forrest/TTT

#16 Nestling under the coal hoist at ALLOA (sub-shed of Dunfermline 62C), NBL 0-4-0 225 h.p. D. H. shunter #D2718 is coupled up to three open wagons loaded with ash clinker during June, 1965.

Norris Forrest/TTT

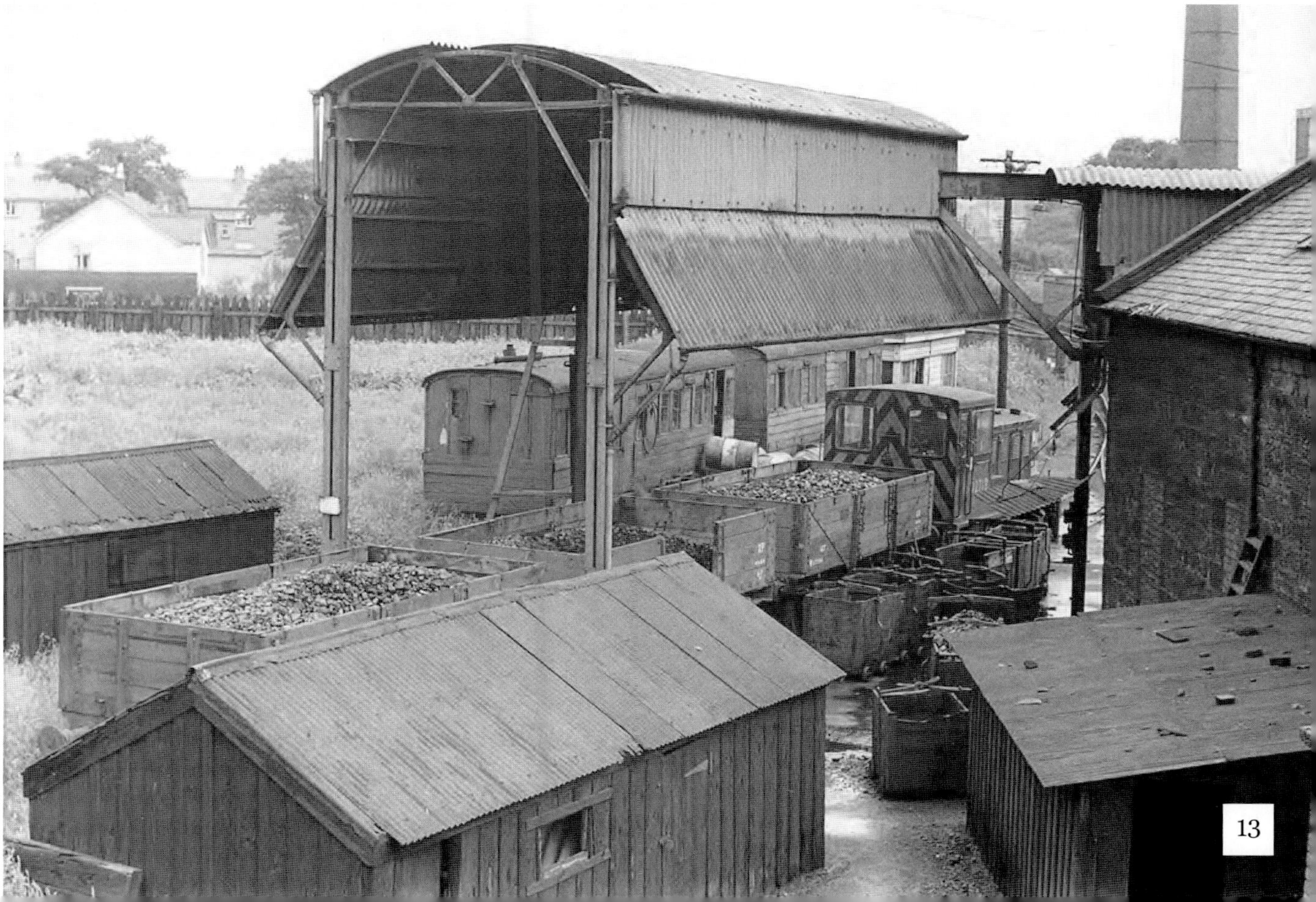

#17 Panoramic view of OBAN (63E) shed in July, 1962 looking towards the junction, during the transition phase from steam to diesel traction. In the distance a pair of unidentified BRCW Type 2 Bo-Bo D.E.s are stabled amid the still functioning ironmongery of a working steam shed with clearly visible the turntable, coaling hopper, coal and fuel oil tank wagons, ash pits and shed buildings. *Alan Carlaw*

#18 Recently introduced to OBAN (63E) loco shed, a reasonably clean unidentified BRCW Type 2 Bo-Bo D.E. undergoes a change of loco crew during the summer of 1963. Note the same four wheel tank wagon still in the same siding a year later. *Ken Nuttall*

PREVIOUS PAGE:
#19 Unidentified EE Type 4 1Co-Co1 D.E. is seen passing ST. MARGARETS (64A) shed on the Up main line on 25th June, 1960. *Ken Nuttall*

#20 (middle) **and #21** (bottom) 2 views of LEITH CENTRAL (sub-shed of St. Margarets) DMU depot on 31st August, 1957 when the location was one of the first converted buildings to service DMUs in Scotland. Seen in both views are powered and unpowered BR Swindon built DMU vehicles. *Robin Nelson (20) and Roy M.B. Crombie/SRPS (21)*

#22 EASTFIELD (65A) loco shed on 18th April 1965 shows a grimy unidentified BRCW Type 2 Bo-Bo D.E. sharing the running roads with four different classes of still active steam locos. *Douglas Hume*

#23 PARKHEAD (65C) shed looking east shows the impressive concrete coaling tower looking like a feature from a science fiction movie as recently introduced BR 0-6-0 350 h.p. D.E. shunter shares the running roads with several classes of ex NBR and LNER steam locomotives. *Roy M.B. Crombie/SRPS*

#24 A panorama of DAWSHOLM (65D) shed on 23rd August, 1961 depicts solitary BR 0-6-0 350 h.p. D.E. shunter in the company of a very mixed bag of ex Caledonian, LMSR and BR standard loco classes. *Douglas Hume*

#25 A close up of a pair of NBL 0-4-0 225 h.p. D.H. shunters #D2770 and #D2765 in seemingly ex-works condition at KIPPS (65E) shed on the 15th October, 1960. Note the four vertical rows of snap headed rivets which connected the locomotive buffer beams to each set of chassis frames behind. *Hamish Stevenson*

#26 POLMADIE (66A) shed during the transition period when the stylish but unreliable Clayton Type 1 Bo-Bo D.E. were being withdrawn. Two unidentified members of the recently introduced distinctive, powerful and reliable fifty members of the EE Type 4 Co-Co D.E. class of main line locomotives can be seen on an adjacent siding. This July 1969 scene depicts that period. *WAC Smith/TTT*

#27 SHIELDHALL (King George V Dock) was a stabling point for Polmadie. Up to six shunters were located here to shunt the rail-connected dock as well as a very extensive marshalling yard and a nearby former shipyard. On 13th July 1976, BR 0-6-0 350 h.p. D.E. shunter #08727 is stabled between shunting duties at the head of the dock, where M.V. DARU 6340 grt launched in 1958 by Scotts S.B. & Eng. Co. Ltd., Greenock for Elder Dempster Lines is being loaded with cargo for West Africa. *Geo. C. O'Hara*

#28 MOTHERWELL (66B) loco shed seen in July 1966, with several BR 0-6-0 350 h.p. D.E. shunters and a pair of unidentified Clayton Type 1 Bo-Bo D.E.s sharing the running roads with several classes of still active steam locos. *Roy M.B. Crombie/SRPS*

#29 Greenock LADYBURN (66D) shed in name only, as the leaking roof provides not much cover from the incessant West of Scotland rain on a March day in 1964. Several BR 0-6-0 350 h.p. D.E. shunters and a solitary Andrew Barclay 205 h.p. D.M. shunter can be seen in this view, sharing the running roads with a pair of 2-6-4 tank locomotives.
Norris Forrest/TTT

#30 Looking almost brand new and just out of the box, BR Type 4 1Co-Co1 D.E. #D24 brings a large dose of modernity to CORKERHILL (67A) shed on 5th May, 1961.
WAC Smith/TTT

#31 A solitary BR 0-6-0 350 h.p. D.E. shunter shares the running roads at HURLFORD (67B) shed on 30th June 1963, when every other adjacent steam locomotive seems to be lit-up and in steam. Two of the former LMSR 4F 0-6-0 locomotives had recently been transferred to Scotland from the L.M. Region.
WAC Smith/TTT

#32 EE Type 4 1Co-Co1 D.E. #40058 makes a smoky exit from AYR (67C) shed where it has been refuelled prior to picking up a speedlink service from Falkland yard to Carlisle on 9th April 1982. The sharply curved line to the left leads to Mauchline via Annbank Junction. Note the rake of four wheel vacuum fitted 16 ton mineral wagons, and the adjacent stacks of domestic coal lying bagged in the former coal merchant siding. *Geo. C. O'Hara*

#33 AYR KYLE STREET (67C) DMU stabling point is shrouded in the exhaust fumes of several different types of DMUs on 11th April 1982. This location was quickly sold-off to a property developer following the electrification of the Ayr line, a few years after this scene was photographed. *Geo. C. O'Hara*

#34 AYR (67C) shed viewed from the south circa 1964 when steam traction still reigned supreme at the depot. A BR 0-6-0 350 h.p. D.E. shunter and a Park Royal 4-wheel diesel railbus share the scene with several ex LMS Class 5 4-6-0 locomotives.
WAC Smith/TTT

#35 EE Type 1 Bo-Bo D.E. #D8086 (depicting tablet catching recess, but bereft of its catcher) is manually turned at the former shed at ARDROSSAN (NORTH) (67D) on 12th July 1963, so that the loco can return cab first to Glasgow.
WAC Smith/TTT

#36 BR Swindon 6-car DMU alongside several steamed and coaled locos at STRANRAER (68C) shed during the summer of 1964. In the foreground with a troop special reporting number is BR std Clan Pacific #72009 Clan Stewart.
WAC Smith/TTT

Section 2
DIESEL RAILBUSES

The concept of developing and operating a lower cost non-locomotive/rolling stock vehicle on the railways of the U.K. was initiated by some of the former railway companies in the form of the steam railcar. These machines were 4-axle hybrids comprising a single rivetted steel chassis containing a steam engine derivative at one end, with a combined passenger/limited luggage carrying capability along the remainder of the frame. A few of these steam railcars worked for several years on some of the lightly used Scottish branch lines prior to nationalisation.

Several European railways, notably West Germany, took this innovative concept further with the development and emergence of various types of 4-wheel diesel railbus designs, utilising underslung bus engines as the power unit for the vehicle, with different types of transmission and gear boxes.

A few types of railbus designs were supplied by a handful of manufacturers to British Railways, and were sent to a dozen or so Scottish lines, all of which were considered to be the right type of location to test their suitability. These railbuses duly remained in Scotland for the remainder of their operating careers to allow the evaluation of this novel type of traction.

Examples of all of the types of railbus which operated on these different Scottish lines are depicted in the photographs in this section. Regrettably, the enthusiastic increase in patronage which quickly followed the railbus introduction, was gradually eroded due to their poor reliability as a result of frequent mechanical failure, and axle breakages. Additionally the giddying effects of noisy over-sensitive suspension, coupled with insufficient horsepower and torque deficient transmission systems on gradients made these units poor performers, although the concept was later revived by British Rail in the 1980s with Classes 140-144.

This selection of photographs depicting railbus operations in Scotland are set out from West to South in a clockwise direction of former routes and services.

LIST OF ROUTES & BRANCH LINE LOCATIONS ILLUSTRATED

#37 Unidentified Park Royal 4-wheel diesel railbus leaves the impressive station, and nearby DMU and coaching stabling sidings at Ardrossan Town with a service to Darvel via Irvine and Kilmarnock on 30th March 1963. *WAC Smith/TTT*

#38 Irvine station and its traditional kiosk provide the location for Park Royal 4-wheel diesel railbus #M79972 on the afternoon service from Ardrossan Town to Darvel on 27th July 1962. *Robin Nelson*

#39 The volcanic cusp of Loudon Hill (1036 ft) provides the backdrop to the Irvine Valley as an unidentified Park Royal 4-wheel diesel railbus leaves the town of Darvel with the afternoon service to Kilmarnock and Irvine on 7th April 1962. Noticeable in the distance are a rake of 16 ton mineral wagons with the station and signal box beyond. WAC *Smith/TTT*

#40 Unidentified Park Royal 4-wheel diesel railbus at Craigendoran setting down passengers from a service from Arrochar & Tarbet on 11th June 1964. *Douglas Hume*

41 Unidentified Park Royal 4-wheel diesel railbus negotiates the sinewy track of the West Highland Railway near the mist shrouded British Petroleum Co. Ltd oil terminal at Finnart on Loch Long with a service from Craigendoran to Arrochar and Tarbet on 28th January 1961. *WAC Smith/TTT*

#42 The remote island platform passing loop and signal box at the now closed station of Glendouglas sees unidentified Park Royal 4-wheel diesel railbus on a Craigendoran to Arrochar and Tarbet service await the arrival of a southbound train in January 1962. *WAC Smith/TTT*

#43 The impressive scissors crossover at Crieff forms an impressive backdrop as an unidentified Park Royal 4-wheel diesel railbus prepares to enter the station of the large Perthshire town on the last day of passenger services on the branch from Gleneagles, 4th July 1964. *Douglas Hume*

#44 The ornate, and under patronised former Caledonian Railway Company station at Crieff on 3rd July 1964 with unidentified Park Royal 4-wheel diesel railbus about to leave on a service to Comrie. *Robin Nelson*

#45 Two young boys, dressed in the fashionable attire of the era, admire D. Wickham 4-wheel diesel railbus #SC79968 at Comrie station on 28th August, 1959, shortly after introduction of the "shoogly" service to Gleneagles via Crieff. *Robin Nelson*

#46 A well patronised D. Wickham 4-wheel diesel railbus #SC79966 is seen at Grantown-on-Spey East station on a service from Boat of Garten to Elgin in July 1960, as an unidentified ex Caledonian Railway '812' class 0-6-0 steam locomotive works the goods service on the line. *WAC Smith/TTT*

#47 Unidentified Park Royal 4-wheel diesel railbus rasps, splutters and 'shoogles' away from Ballindalloch with a service from Keith Junction to Aviemore in June 1965. *Roy M.B. Crombie/SRPS*

#48 Craigellachie on 9th August 1962 with D. Wickham 4-wheel diesel railbus #SC79969 ready to leave with a service to Aviemore.
Robin Nelson

#49 Park Royal 4-wheel diesel railbus #SC79967 is a wee bit mottled by early evening shadows at Craigellachie before leaving for Aviemore on 22nd July 1964.
Hamish Stevenson

#50 D. Wickham 4-wheel diesel railbus #SC79969 outside Craigellachie with a service along the Spey valley to Aviemore on 9th August 1962. Note the line to Elgin via Rothes beyond.
Robin Nelson

#51 and #52 Author's licence is deployed here to create a fabricated composition of a 'mock railbus working' on the former Aberfeldy branch. These two views depict an over-powered train consist of diesel locomotive hauling a suburban brake coach in the Tay valley. #51 (top) shows BR Type 2 Bo-Bo D.E. #D5123 approaching Aberfeldy with the mid-day service from Ballinluig Junction. #52 (bottom) shows the same train formation somewhere near Grandtully with the return service from Aberfeldy to Ballinluig Junction during March 1965, two months before complete closure of the scenic Perthshire branch line. *Both photos: Roy Hamilton*

#53 Unidentified Park Royal 4-wheel diesel railbus passes the private siding to the world famous Gleneagles Hotel with a service from Gleneagles to Crieff in June 1964.
Douglas Hume

#54 The impressive station at Gleneagles is about to be departed by an unidentified D. Wickham 4-wheel diesel railbus with a service to Crieff and Comrie on 2nd January 1960.
WAC Smith/TTT

#55 Park Royal 4-wheel diesel railbus #M79971 takes the line for Grangemouth at Grange-mouth Junction, Falkirk with a service to the Forth Port on 20th January 1968.
Robin Nelson

#56 Bristol/ Eastern Coach Works 4-wheel diesel railbus #SC79959 is seen at the island platform of Strathaven Central with a service for Hamilton on 20th May 1960.

J.N. Faulkner

#57 Park Royal 4-wheel diesel railbus #SC79974 leaves Hollybush with a service from Kilmarnock to Dalmellington via Ayr in May 1961.

Roy M.B. Crombie/SRPS

#58 Park Royal 4-wheel diesel railbus #SC79974 shoogles so much that its destination board is blurred as it rattles past the site of the former Potterston Junction and the long closed branch to Coylton Colliery with a service from Dalmellington to Ayr on 30th January 1960.

WAC Smith/TTT

#59 Gloucester R.C. & W. Co. diesel railcar #SC55007 passes St. Marnock signal box and adjacent goods yard with a substitute diesel railbus service from Ayr to Kilmarnock on 22nd February 1960. *Douglas Hume*

#60 Park Royal 4-wheel diesel railbus #SC79977 serves the basic halt at Throsk to decant a single passenger from a Larbert to Alloa service on 20th January 1968, shortly before withdrawal of this service. *Robin Nelson*

#61 Bristol/Easter Coach Works wheel diesel railbu #SC79958 passes rake of stored ar antiquated 4-whe goods vans outsic the former station Beith with a servic for Lugton on 15 September 1961.
Douglas Hum

#62 AC 4-wheel diesel railbus #SC79976 leaves Beith Town station, former engine shed, goods yard and adjacent spread of traditional factories with a service for Lugton in June 1961.
Roy M.B. Crombie/SRPS

#63 Bristol/Eastern Coach Works 4-whee diesel railbus #SC7995 east of the village o Barrmill with a Beith Town to Lugton servic on 15th Septembe 1961. *Douglas Hum*

#64 Park Royal 4-wheel diesel railbus #SC79972 arrives at Dollar on the Devon valley line after working a service from Stirling in June 1964. The sight of the tail light above one of the buffers indicates that a shunting operation is taking place.
WAC Smith/TTT

#65 Unidentified D. Wickham 4-wheel diesel railbus approaches Dollar with a service from Stirling in September 1963. Note the row of new houses in the distance. These were built in the 1950s to house miners who were being transferred from other parts of the Scottish coalfields to work in new pits then being sunk in the county of Clackmannan.
Roy M.B. Crombie/SRPS

#66 D. Wickham 4-wheel diesel railbus #SC79966 passes the former locomotive shed at Alloa where several steam engines are stabled with a service from Dunfermline Upper to Stirling in September 1963. *WAC Smith/TTT*

Section 3

DIESEL MULTIPLE UNITS

In advance of the government's approval of the British Railways Modernisation Plan of 1955 was the sanction, development and manufacture of several types of Diesel Multiple Units, or state of the art carriages powered by underslung modified bus engines and bogie mounted transmissions. Such was the perceived demand for the thousands of these revolutionary railcars, that seven established private railway rolling stock builders, and four major B.R. workshops at Derby, Swindon, Ashford and Eastleigh worked on this mammoth project to re-equip the national railway system well into the 1960's.

All of these new D.M.U's were strikingly modern. They were comfortable, fast, cleaner on the inside, spacious, and although often noisy, and with varying degrees of rattle, they were well received by passengers and operating personnel throughout the entire BR network. Inevitably some classes of D.M.U. were more reliable than others. Scotland got a good share of these brand new types of traction, with delivery from several different builders providing part of its urban and rural network with gleaming examples of different types of this new type of train.

Remarkably the B.R. Design Panel and the design offices of the different classes of DMU builders produced several strikingly different front end configurations of their respective vehicles, which were all built on a standard 63'0" fabricated steel chassis with basically similar styles of windows, flush fitting doors, and engines and transmissions manufactured by established British bus builders.

This first generation of DMU's served Scotland very well, especially the ubiquitous sets of units designed and built by Metro-Cammell Ltd. These vehicles lasted for nearly four decades in front line high utilisation service, and became synonymous with the Scottish Railway network during that period. Even the application of overdue somewhat gaudy and tacky livery rebranding did not detract from their iconic style and impressive reliability.

LIST OF LOCATIONS ILLUSTRATED

#67 Two BR Swindon 3-car DMUs forming a six-car Inter City formation stop at Forres in August 1970 with an Inverness to Aberdeen service not long after the station was reduced to a single platform. *Geo. C. O'Hara*

#68 Cravens 2-car DMU leaves the quaintly named and truly rustic Spey Bay station with an Elgin to Aberdeen service via Buckie on 21st May 1966. *Jack Kernahan*

#69 The soft tones of the northern summer evening sky provide a fine coastal shimmering haze as Cravens 2-car DMU leaves Portgordon with an Elgin to Cairnie Junction service in July 1965. *Roy M.B. Crombie/SRPS*

#70 Metro-Cammell 2-car DMU at the basic single platform station of St. Combs with a service for Fraserburgh on 21st November 1963. *John M. Boyes – The Armstrong Railway Photographic Trust*

#71 Cravens 2-car DMU stops at the wayside halt and former station and goods yard of Cairnbulg on 21st September, 1963 with a service from Fraserburgh. *Douglas Hume*

#72 BR Swindon 3-car DMU passes under Union Street bridge in the heart of Scotland's famous Granite City with a service from Aberdeen to Inverness in June 1977.
WAC Smith/TTT

#73 A close-up of BR Swindon 3-car DMU in Aberdeen in June 1970. These stylish DMUs gave two decades of comfortable and reliable service on the line to Inverness, and their introduction led to greater use of the railway in this part of Scotland.
John M. Boyes – The Armstrong Railway Photographic Trust

#74 Fraserburgh station on 3rd April 1965 with NBL Type 2 Bo-Bo D.E. #D6145 on a service to Aberdeen, and a 2-car Cravens DMU in front of a 2-car Metro-Cammell DMU in the adjacent platform with a service to St. Combs.
Douglas Hume

#75 Unusual combination of what looks like a pair of pristine Cravens 2-car DMUs crossing over at Longside on the Peterhead branch. Such a meeting so near the terminus station is probably due to crew training on 4th July 1959.
Roy Hamilton

#76 Cravens 2-car DMU makes a smoky departure from Craigellachie with a service for Elgin via Rothes in October 1967. Note the very basic yet distinctive and austere GNSR footbridge which was a common structure at stations in the north east of Scotland. *G.N. Turnbull*

#77 Mist shrouded tidy and well kept Ballater station and adjacent though run-down goods yard seems too grand a venue for 2-car Cravens DMU ready to leave on a service to Aberdeen on 9th October 1965. *Douglas Hume*

#78 Iconic and hyper-powered HST storms away from Montrose with an Aberdeen to London Kings Cross service on 16th October, 1980.
Geo. C. O'Hara

#79 Scotch mist obliterates the rugged profile of the mountains of Breadalbane as a Cravens 6 car DMU crawls over the castellated stone-work of the River Dochart viaduct at Killin with a Six Lochs diesel land cruise service during March 1960.
WAC Smith/TTT

#80 BR Swindon 3-car DMU heads towards Loch Tay, to allow the arrival of the steam hauled branch line train to enter Killin station on 19th May 1960. *Robin Nelson*

#81 The singl platform at Killi station is throngin with passengers from BR Cravens 6-car DMU on a Six Lochs diese land cruise to th pleasant Perthshir village on 30th Ma 1959. *WAC Smith/TT*

#82 A south-bound 7-car hybrid Six Lochs diesel land cruise headed by BR Derby 3-car DMU crosses over one of the bowstring girder bridges in the Pass of Leny a few miles north of Callander during July 1961. *WAC Smith/TTT*

#83 The north end o Callander station on 21st August 1960, with what appears to be two separate Six Lochs land cruise workings both made up o Cravens 6-car DMUs occupying the up and down platforms. *WAC Smith/TTT*

84 Metro-Cammell 2-car MU at Crieff on 16th July, 1956. This unit was from the Eastern egion allocation and was on valuation service on the erthshire branch.
WAC Smith/TTT

85 Metro-Cammell 2-car MU passes by the western hore of Loch Leven with an dinburgh Waverley to Perth ervice via Glenfarg on 15th November 1969. *Douglas Hume*

86 A 3-car Metro-Cammell MU in a hybrid mixture of BR reen and rail blue liveries rasps way from St. Andrews with a ervice for Leuchars Junction on th January 1969. *G.N. Turnbull*

#87 Metro-Cammell 3-car DMU rattles past the remains of Milnathort station and surviving goods yard with a Perth to Edinburgh Waverley service via Glenfarg on 13th December 1969, shortly before complete closure of this route.
Douglas Hume

#88 Metro-Cammell 3-car DMU splutters away from Leven with a service for Edinburgh Waverley on 28th August, 1965, a few days before closure of the through route to St. Andrews via the Fife Coast Line. *Douglas Hume*

#89 The intricate structure and web of inter-lacing diagonal steel bracing nicely frame Gloucester R.C. & W. Co. 2-car DMU as it crosses over the iconic nineteenth century engineering marvel that is the Forth Bridge with a service for Edinburgh Waverley from Kirkcaldy on 13th November 1971. *Jack Kernahan*

#90 Hybrid 2-car DMU with a Metro-Cammell vehicle trailing behind a Gloucester R.C. and W. Co. unit, leaves Drem with a service for North Berwick in June 1972. Note the impressive rust free rivetted water tower still intact some five or six years after steam working ended in Scotland, and the rake of vans in the adjacent goods yard. *G.N.Turnbull*

#91 Gloucester R.C. & Co. 4-car near Drem Juncti with a service for Edinbur Waverley on 20th Augu 1960. Note the cusp of t volcanic crag known as t 'North Berwick Law' (613 on the horizon.
WAC Smith/T

#92 Gloucester R.C. & W. Co. 2-car DMU at the former tidy Edinburgh suburban station of Duddingston (for Craigmillar) with a service to Rosewell and Hawthornden on 25th August 1962.
Roy Hamilton

#93 BR Swindon car DMU accelerat out of Edinbur Waverley with inter-city service Glasgow Queen Stre on 3rd April 1971.
G.N.Turnb

#94 BR Swindon 6-car DMU in blue and grey livery passes the large former coal yard at Haymarket with an inter-city service for Glasgow Queen Street on 3rd April 1971. *G.N.Turnbull*

#95 Metro-Cammell 3-car DMU (in the bay platform with a service for Grangemouth), is overtaken in Polmont station by ex LNER A2 class 4-6-2 #60536 'Trimbush' hauling the North Briton Pullman car train on the 'down' line in January 1963. *WAC Smith/TTT*

#96 Gloucester R.C. & W. Co. 4-car DMU near a snow covered Fauldhouse with an Edinburgh Princes Street to Glasgow Central service on 12th January 1963. *WAC Smith/TTT*

2H

A

PREVIOUS PAGE:

#97 Several bings of spoil from the Lanarkshire collieries around Fauldhouse form the industrial backdrop to a BR Swindon 6 car DMU service from a diverted Glasgow Central to Edinburgh Waverley via Shotts in November 1960. *Roy M.B. Crombie/SRPS*

#98 Metro-Cammell 3-car DMU near the triangular track configuration of Carmuirs East Junction with a service from Grangemouth to Stirling on 1st September 1964. *Robin Nelson*

#99 BR Swindon 6-car DMU approaches Falkirk High and passes ex-NBR/LNER Y9 0-4-0 'pug' on shunting duties, whilst on a driver training service between Glasgow and Edinburgh on 9th March 1957. *Robin Nelson*

#100 BR Super sprinter #158.704/7 in attractive but easily weathered Express livery passes a track repair crew welding a crossover near Greenhill Lower Junction on 10th February 1991 while working a Glasgow Queen Street to Edinburgh Waverley service. *Max Fowler*

#101 BR Swindon 6-car DMU passes through Cumbernauld with a driver training working in July 1959, when the location was pock marked with traditional factories and before the sprawl of the new town was built. *Roy M.B. Crombie/SRPS*

#102 Metro Cammell 3-car DMU near Middlemuir Junction, Lenzie with a service from Kirkintilloch to Glasgow Queen Street on 10th May 1960. *Robin Nelson*

#103 Cravens 4-car DMU near Hamilton West with a service from Glasgow Central on 2nd March 1963. The lattice-framed girder over bridge carried the former NB line to Bothwell.
WAC Smith/TTT

#104 Derby 3-car DMU at Larkhall Central station with a Coalburn to Glasgow Central service in February 1962, some three years before the passenger service was withdrawn from the former Lanarkshire mining town, only to be re-instated over four decades later!
Norris Forrest/TTT

#105 Metro-Cammell 2-car DMU crosses the former six span Sandilands bowstring girder viaduct over the Douglas Water, a tributary of the River Clyde with a service from Douglas West to Lanark on 12th September 1964.

Douglas Hume

#106 Cravens 2-car DMU enters Ponfeigh with a service from Muirkirk to Lanark in April 1963. Note the rake of empty 16 ton mineral wagons for nearby Douglas Colliery (the most southerly pit in the former Lanarkshire coal field), which closed after a fire in September 1967.

Roy M.B. Crombie/SRPS

#107 Cravens 2-car DMU near the site of the former Bothwell Castle Junction with a service from Strathaven to Glasgow Central in August 1965.

Roy M.B. Crombie/SRPS

#108 Signalman and the driver of Metro-Cammell 2-car DMU on a Coalburn to Stonehouse service exchange tablets at Alton Heights signal box on 20th May 1964. This large former Caledonian Railway box once controlled four adjoining lines, all constructed to transport the outputs from the once very productive nearby Lanarkshire coalfield. *John Spencer Gilks*

#109 BR Derby 3-car Suburban DMU rasps away from East Kilbride with a service for Glasgow Central on 23rd February 1974, the last day of manual signalling on the branch. At this time the branch still had a daily pick-up goods service.

WAC Smith/TTT

#110 Metro-Cammell 6-car DMU leaves a dark and gloomy Rutherglen, with a service for Glasgow Central in November 1960, where the adjacent and busy coal yard contains many four-wheel wooden body wagons

Roy M.B. Crombie/SRPS

#111 Framed by a still operational water crane and brazier, Derby 6-car DMU leaves Glasgow St. Enoch with a local service for Carlisle via the Nith valley line, just as the snow begins to fall in January 1966. *Jack Kernahan*

#112 BR Swindon 6-car DMU has just crossed over the Clyde Bridge Viaduct with a service to Ayr from Glasgow St. Enoch on 6th June 1966. *Robin Nelson*

#113 BR Derby 6-car DMU crawls through the closed Cumberland Street station with a service from Ayr to Glasgow St. Enoch on 6th June 1966. *Robin Nelson*

#114 Hybrid DMU consist with a Gloucester R.C. & W.Co vehicle leading, passes through Pollokshields East with a Glasgow Central to Neilston service on 9th January 1960. Note the Glasgow Corporation Transport Dept tramways works to the right. *WAC Smith/TTT*

#115 The combination of railway architecture and ironmongery of signalling and electrification masts and catenaries nicely frame a Cravens 2-car DMU as it leaves Maxwell Park with a Cathcart Inner Circle service on 2nd February 1961.
WAC Smith/TTT

#116 Metro-Cammell 2-car DMU approaches Partick West Junction with a service bound for Dalmuir Riverside on the misty 30th September 1964.
Robin Nelson

#117 Hybrid 4-car DMU consisting of Metro-Cammell 2-car unit and Cravens 2-car unit traiIling passes the spur connection to the Clydeside Tramway beyond Partick East Junction with an eastbound service on the 30th September 1964. *Robin Nelson*

#118 Metro-Cammell 2-car DMU leads a Cravens 2-car DMU from the Maryhill Central line past part of the former triangular junction at Partick East signal box on 30th September 1964 with a service for Rutherglen via Glasgow Central Low Level. *Robin Nelson*

#119 Cravens 4-car DMU rattles through the closed site of the former Kelvinside station with a Coatbridge to Possil service on 25th September 1964, shortly before withdrawal of the passenger service on this suburban line which had several miles of tunnels under some of the districts of the City of Glasgow. *Douglas Hume*

#120 Partick Central signal box, and the buildings and siding of the former Spillers Ltd flour mill at Partick provide an interesting background for a Cravens 2-car DMU crossing over the River Kelvin and about to enter Kelvinhaugh tunnel with a Dalmuir Riverside to Rutherglen service via Glasgow Central Low Level on 2nd October 1964. *Roy Hamilton*

#121 Metro-Cammell 3-car DMU leads a 5 car hybrid combination near Upper Greenock with a service for Wemyss Bay during December 1964. At this point the railway is several hundred feet above the nearby River Clyde. *Norris Forrest/TTT*

#122 BR Derby 3-car DMU in hybrid rail blue and blue/grey livery variations speeds towards Kilmacolm with an afternoon service from Glasgow Central on 5th April 1980.
Geo. C. O'Hara

#123 BR Derby 3-car DMU now carrying Tops class 116 prefix purrs along between Mosspark West and Crookston with a Glasgow Central to Kilmacolm service on 25th March 1982. *Tom H Noble*

#124 Gloucester R.C. & W. Co. single diesel railcar #SC55013 substitutes for a failed 3-car DMU with a Glasgow-Kilmarnock service on 16th April 1984, and is seen climbing Neilston bank at Shilford, where the track has recently been singled and re-ballasted.
Geo C. O'Hara

#125 Gloucester R. C. & W. Co. 4-car DMU at Renfrew Fulbar Street with a service from Renfrew Wharf to Glasgow Central in July 1967, a few weeks before withdrawal of the passenger railway service.
Jack Kernahan

#126 Cravens 2-car DMU depicts a remarkably mottled effect of autumnal lighting on its BR green livery as it purrs away from Barrhead bound for Kilmarnock with a service from Glasgow Central in September 1968. *Jack Kernahan*

#127 BR Swindon 6-car DMU near Lochwinnoch (St. Brydes) with a Glasgow St. Enoch to Ayr via Kilbirnie service on 30th July 1963, when this former line provided a duplicate route through the Upper Garnock valley, and rejoined the main line to Ayr at Brownhill Junction, north of Dalry. *WAC Smith/TTT*

#128 BR Derby 3-car DMU accelerates away from Glengarnock with a service from Largs to Glasgow Central on 11th May 1981. Note the rake of vaccum fitted plate wagons in the adjacent siding, indicating that rail borne raw and finished steel products were still being transported to the nearby B.S.C. Glengarnock Rolling Mill. *Geo. C. O'Hara*

#129 Cravens 2-car DMU at Uplawmoor on 30th March 1962 with a service about to depart for Glasgow Central, on the last day of operation from this station. This former Caledonian Railway route once ran to Kilwinning, but was cut back to Neilston on this same day of curtailment. *Roy Hamilton*

130 Metro-Cammell 3-car DMU splutters past the signal box on the approach to Largs station with a service from Glasgow Central in the afternoon of 27th January 1984, shortly before the line was electrified and partly singled from Ardrossan. *Geo. C. O'Hara*

#131 Gloucester R.C. & W. Co. 2-car DMU leaves Montgreenan and crosses over the Lugton Water with a Glasgow St. Enoch to Kilmarnock via Dalry service on 29th December 1965. This route was later closed and lifted in the early 1970s. *Douglas Hume*

#132 Faltering and spluttering BR Swindon 3-car DMU gets 'tender first' banking assistance from ex-LNER B1 4-6-0- #61197 near Maybole whilst on a service from Girvan to Glasgow St. Enoch on 7th June 1963. *Derek Cross*

#133 BR Derby 3-car DMU now carrying Tops class 107 prefix trundles past the location of a tidy looking Ayr loco shed with a service bound for Glasgow Central on 10th August 1984, shortly before the line was electrified. *Geo. C. O'Hara*

#134 BR Swindon 3-car DMU speeds through the arable Ayrshire countryside near Maybole with a Stranraer to Glasgow Central service on 23rd February 1979.
Geo. C. O'Hara

#135 A pair of BR Derby class 156 sprinter DMUs pass Dalrymple Junction with a service from Newcastle to Stranraer on 21st June 1990. The line to the left is the freight only branch to Waterside open cast coal loading point.
Geo. C. O'Hara

#136 Gloucester R.C. & W. Co. 2-car DMU leaves the basic single platform halt at the sonorously named Cardrona in the picturesque valley of the River Tweed with a service from Galashiels to Edinburgh Waverley via Peebles on 18th November 1961.
WAC Smith/TTT

#137 Gloucester R.C. & W. Co. 2-car DMU stops at Innerleithen where the goods yard is still functional, with a service from Galashiels to Edinburgh Waverley via Peebles on 11th November 1961.
WAC Smith/TTT

#138 Metro-Cammell 3-car DMU between Stow and Fountainhall with a Hawick to Edinburgh Waverley stopping service on 17th August 1968. The generous sweeping curves and impeccable parallel geometry of the track at this location clearly indicate the excellence of the permanent way of the former Waverley Route.
G.N. Turnbull

#139 BR Swindon 3-car DMU in the improved livery of blue and grey, and with the angular GG logo and Tops class 126 classification speeds past Auldgirth, near Dumfries with an Ayr-Carlisle service on 22nd September 1973.
Tom H. Noble

Section 4

LOCOMOTIVE HAULED PASSENGER TRAINS

The transition from steam locomotive hauled passenger trains was basically the substitution of a different type of motive power traction, which took about a decade to be fully implemented. The optimism expected from this changeover for improved timings and sustainable reliability was never fully achieved until the Brush Type 4 Co-Co, and EE Type 3 Co-Co diesel electric locomotives became widespread throughout the Scottish Region.

The number of different varieties of Type 2 Bo-Bo D.E. locomotives were all basically under-powered by about 50% for the arduous operational duty cycles which B.R. planners envisaged. Despite their collective under-powered characteristics, only the Glasgow built N.B.L. Type 2 Bo-Bo D.E's gave such a chronic catalogue of unreliability that the entire class of nearly 60 engines was withdrawn from service by 1971. The B.R., and B.R.C.W. Type 2 Sulzer engine Bo-Bo D.E's were synonymous with the entire Scottish Region for nearly 30 years. Their distinctive mellifluous syncopating throaty bark is nowadays no longer heard resonating from the glens, cuttings, embankments and stations where they once hauled trains which always seemed too long to be pulled by these wee diesels. The iconic E.E. Type 5 Co-Co Deltic class of 22 D.E. locomotives spent their entire career on the east coast of Scotland, hauling express passenger services from Edinburgh to London Kings Cross and latterly as far north as Aberdeen before their withdrawal in 1982.

LIST OF LOCATIONS ILLUSTRATED

140 BRCW Type 2 Bo-Bo D.E. #D5330 restarts an Inverness to Wick & Thurso passenger service from Lairg in June 1966. Note the Royal Mail Travelling Post Office coach next to the locomotive, an EE Type 1 Bo-Bo D.E. in the goods yard, and the photographer's Triumph Herald car. *Roy M.B. Crombie/SRPS*

141 BRCW Type 2 Bo-Bo D.E.s #26038 and 26032 climb away from Georgemas Junction with the evening Wick & Thurso combined service to Inverness on 4th July 1984. Up until 1981 this working usually conveyed at least one Blue Spot insul fish van between the second locomotive and the first passenger coach. *Tom H. Noble*

142 The magnificent mountain profile of the Isle of Skye is seen to good effect in this rustic railway composition as BRCW Type2 Bo-Bo D.E. #26030 heads a three coach train for Inverness, a few miles east of Kyle of Lochalsh on 5th October, 1982. A feature of the modus operandi of the lines north of Inverness was the regular positioning of BG vans in the middle of these trains. *Tom H. Noble*

#143 Unidentified BR Type 2 Bo-Bo D.E. about to leave Kyle of Lochalsh for Inverness with a service containing as many parcel vans as passenger coaches in May 1975. Note the number of vans and wagons in the adjacent sidings on either side of the station. *Roy M.B. Crombie/SRPS*

#144 Unidentified BRCW Type 2 Bo-Bo D.E. splutters away from Garve where the station still provides a working goods yard, with a lengthy train from Inverness to Kyle of Lochalsh during June 1965. *Roy M.B. Crombie/SRPS*

#145 NBL Type 2 Bo-Bo D.E. #D6146 passes under the impressive semaphore signal gantry at the east end of Inverness with a service for Keith Junction on 16th June 1962. The train formation contains several passenger coaches built before the establishment of British Railways.

WAC Smith/TTT

#146 BR Type 2 Bo-Bo D.E. #D5128 descends the wooded valley south of Dava Summit with an Inverness to Glasgow Buchanan Street via Forres service in June 1965.

Roy M.B. Crombie/SRPS

#147 BRCW Type 2 Bo-Bo D.E. #D5336 crosses over the River Spey and enters Craigellachie with an over-powered one coach 'rail bus substitute' service from Elgin to Aviemore in June 1965.

Roy M.B. Crombie/SRPS

#148 BRCW Type 2 Bo-Bo D.E. #D5341 stops at Cromdale with a one coach train from Elgin to Aviemore during June 1964. The locomotive driver and second man take some time to watch the train guard wrestle with some parcels from an antiquated wheel barrow. *David Sleight/GNSRA*

#149 Unidentified NBL Type 2 Bo-Bo D.E. stops at Elgin where the extensive station canopy can be seen to good effect with a service via the coast line bound for Inverness sometime in March 1963. *Norris Forrest/TTT*

#150 NBL Type 2 Bo-Bo D.E. #D6141 on the reverse curve approach to Lossiemouth station and goods yard with a train from Elgin on 4th April 1964.
Roy Hamilton

#151 Passengers alight and parcels are unloaded at Lossiemouth from a short train from Elgin hauled by NBL Type 2 Bo-Bo D.E. #D6141 on 4th April 1964, the last day of passenger services on the branch. Noticeable below the station clock on the left, is the famous bell which was rung for all departing trains from the former Morayshire station.
Roy Hamilton

CGG 318

PREVIOUS PAGE:
#152 NBL Type 2 Bo-Bo D.E. #D6156 pauses at the tiny single platform station of Portgordon with a two coach service from Elgin to Buckie on 28th April 1961. *Douglas Hume*

#153 BR Type 2 Bo-Bo D.E. #D5116 enters Portessie with an Elgin to Aberdeen via Buckie service in July 1966. Note the trackbed of the former HR to Keith via Aultmore on the left. *Roy Hamilton*

#154 Unidentified NBL Type 2 Bo-Bo D.E. leaves an almost deserted Cullen with a short train from Keith Junction to Elgin via Buckie in June 1965. Note the photographer's Triumph Herald car parked on the street. *Roy M.B. Crombie/SRPS*

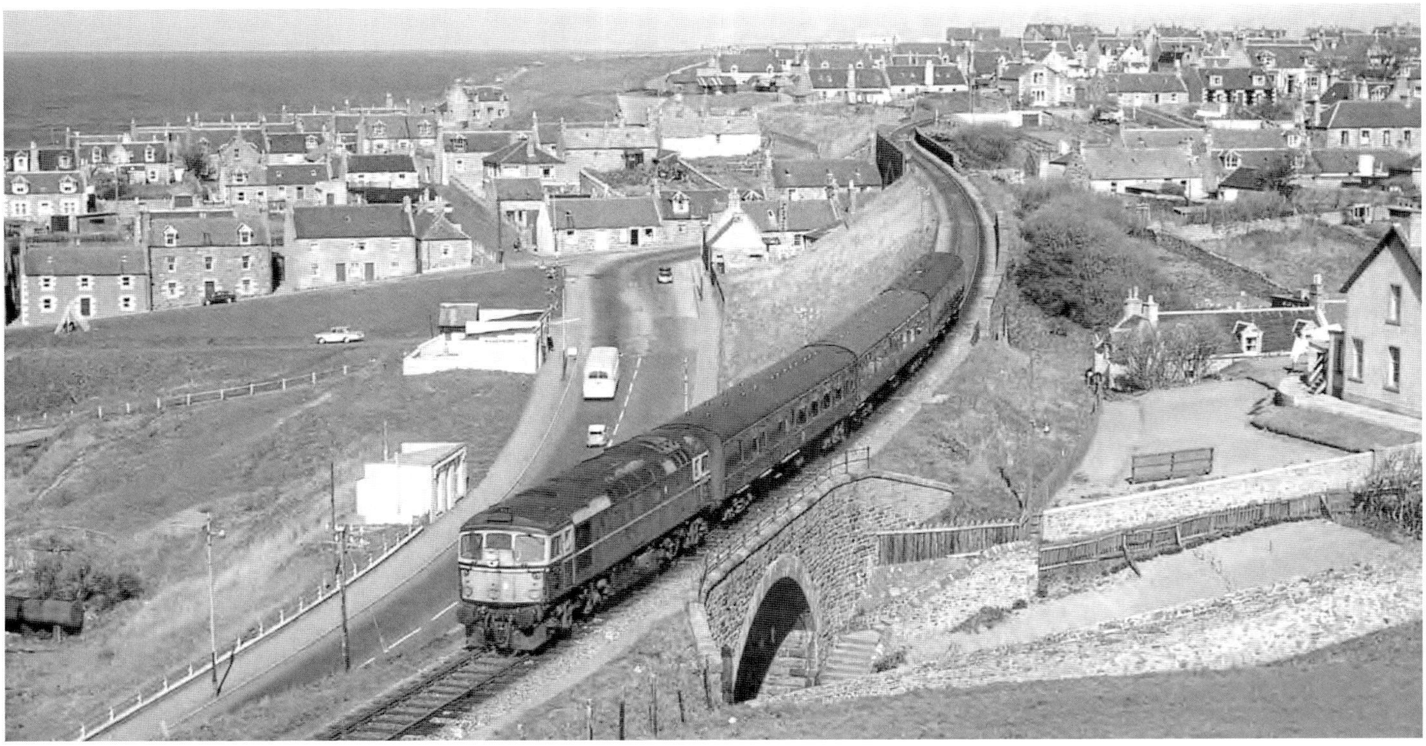

#155 Unidentified BRCW Type 2 Bo-Bo D.E. leaves the imposing seaside town of Cullen with a service from Buckie to Elgin on 7th May 1966. The elevated route with several viaducts and bridges, built by the former GNSR afforded excellent views of the town and the Moray Firth beyond. *Mike Stephen – GNSRA*

#156 Looking almost brand new, NBL Type 2 Bo-Bo D.E. #D6155 arrives at Craigellachie with a service from Elgin to Aberdeen via the Glen Route on 1st April 1961. The second coach in this train formation is a twelve wheeled ex-LMSR Restaurant Car. *Hamish Stevenson*

#157 NBL Type 2 Bo-Bo D.E. #D6141 at Fraserburgh with a service for Aberdeen on 21st April 1962. Note the adjacent two road engine shed, and the widespread use of Aberdeenshire granite in the construction of the surrounding buildings.
Robin Nelson

#158 NBL Type 2 Bo-Bo DE. #D6136 on a passenger service to Peterhead spurts out a vulcanous amount of exhaust plume, as she passes unidentified sister locomotive on a mixed goods for Kittybrewester yard at Longside in June 1965.
Sandy Murdoch/TTT

NEXT PAGE:
#159 Maud Junction on 21st April 1962 with NBL Type 2 Bo-Bo D.E. #D6141 to the left, and sister locomotive #D6142 to the right on trains from Fraserburgh and Peterhead respectively. *Robin Nelson*

#160 EE Type 1 Bo-Bo D.E. #D8029 shunts the yard at Maud Junction where several Blue Spot insul fish vans can be seen in one of the sidings, as a pair of unidentified NBL Type 2 Bo-Bo D.E.s get the right of way with a train for Aberdeen in June 1964. *Sandy Murdoch/TTT*

#161 BR Large logo Brush Type 4 Co-Co D.E. #47460 near Kinaldie on the south bank of the River Don with a four coach service from Aberdeen to Inverness on 2nd June 1988.
Geo. C. O'Hara

PREVIOUS PAGE:

#162 EE Type 4 1Co-Co1 D.E. #D365 passes under the spectacular sets of signal gantries outside Aberdeen station with a service for Glasgow Buchanan Street via the Strathmore route in the mid-1960's. *Jack Kernahan*

#163 NBL Type 2 Bo-Bo D.E. #D6145 restarts an Aberdeen bound service from Forfar sometime in June 1965. *Norris Forrest/TTT*

#164 EE Type 4 1Co-Co1 D.E. #D361 arrives at Forfar with an Aberdeen to Glasgow Buchanan Street service in August 1967, shortly before closure of the Strathmore line as a through route to passenger services. *Norris Forrest/TTT*

#165 NBL Type 2 Bo-Bo D.E. #D6102 stops at Alyth Junction with a lengthy mixed rake of maroon, and blue and grey liveried BR Mk1 coaches bound for Aberdeen in August 1967, by which time the service had departed from Glasgow Queen Street. *Norris Forrest/TTT*

#166 Unusual motive power in the form of BR Type 4 1Co-Co1 D.E. #46033 arrives at Montrose with a service from Aberdeen to Edinburgh Waverley on 5th March 1981. *Mike Cooper – GNSRA*

#167 The cranes of the famous Burntisland Shipbuilding Co. Ltd, provide part of the backdrop for BRCW Type 2 Bo-Bo D.E. #D5309 as it skirts the north shore of the Firth of Forth with a service for Edinburgh Waverley from Aberdeen in June 1965.

WAC Smith/TTT

#168 Steam leaks from a few of the suburban coaches of a Grangemouth to Glasgow Buchanan Street service as mint condition BRCW Type 2 Bo-Bo D.E. #D5349 awaits the right of way from the Stirlingshire port on 25th November 1961.

WAC Smith/TTT

#169 NBL Type 2 Bo-Bo D.E. #D6104 slows down to stop at Gleneagles with a service from Dundee Tay Bridge to Glasgow Buchanan Street in July 1966. By this time the location had ceased to be a junction, a fact evinced by the removal of the "Crieff line" arm from the signal post on the station platform.

Sandy Murdoch/TTT

#170 A pair of NBL Type 2 Bo-E D.E.s #D6134 and #D6136 power service from Dundee West to Glasgo Buchanan Street near Greenh Junction on 16th February 1963.
WAC Smith/T

#171 NBL Type 2 Bo-Bo D.E. #D61 passes through Bridge of Allan with Aberdeen to Glasgow Buchanan Stre service on 10th June 1966.
Derek Cro

#172 NBL Type 2 Bo-Bo D #D6110 and a four coach rake of ve mixed suburban stock with LNER a LMSR types in the consist, passes ne Ross Junction with a service f Glasgow Central on 13th July 1962.
Geo. H. Rol

BINNS DEPOSITORY

PREVIOUS PAGE:
#173 Unidentified EE Type 1 Bo-Bo DE. is about to pass Dalry Road engine shed where three open wagons have tidily been filled with firebox ash on 14th August 1965, whilst hauling a service from Edinburgh Princes Street to the Butlins Holiday camp on the Heads of Ayr branch. *Roy Hamilton*

#174 A pair of unidentified and already quite grimy Clayton Type 1 Bo-Bo D.E.s roar past the tenements of Merchiston with an Edinburgh Princes Street to Liverpool Exchange service on 14th August 1965. Note the lines of washing 'hanging-out' in the 'back greens' of the houses. *Roy Hamilton*

BELOW:
#175 Displaying the world famous "Flying Scotsman" headboard, EE Deltic Type 5 Co-Co D.E. #D9000 'Royal Scots Grey' makes a characteristic and volcanic double plume of engine exhaust as it departs from Edinburgh Waverley on 18th June 1962. *W.S. Sellar*

NEXT PAGE:
#176 EE Deltic Type 5 Co-Co DE. #55010 'The Kings Own Scottish Borderer' glides along the clifftops near Burnmouth with a London Kings Cross to Edinburgh Waverley express on 18th August 1981. *Morrison Bryce*

#177 EE Type 4 1Co-Co1 D.E. #D248 approaches the wayside station of Grantshouse with a three coach Edinburgh Waverley to Berwick-on-Tweed stopping service on 19th August 1961. *WAC Smith/TTT*

#178 Craigentinny yard sees first generation dieselisation on 16th April 1960 with EE Type 4 1Co-Co1 D.E. #D261 heading north on a parcels service whilst a pair of unidentified BRCW Type 2 Bo-Bo D.E.s wait to take some empty stock towards Edinburgh Waverley. *Ken Falconer*

#179 BRCW Type 2 Bo-Bo D.E. #D5351 shunts the stock of a railtour special at Mallaig in the early 1960s. The three rail mounted steam cranes and several insulated containers on conflat wagons indicate that railborne fish traffic still had a few years of revenue earning service to perform from this West Highland railhead. *Alan Carlaw*

#180 Unidentified BRCW Type 2 Bo-Bo D.E. emerges from one of the tunnels blasted out of the rocky hillside, near Loch-Nan-Uamh and crosses the viaduct at the head of the loch, with a Mallaig to Glasgow service in June 1967. *Roy M.B. Crombie/SRPS*

#181 NBL Type 2 Bo-Bo D.E. #D6133 enters Glenfinnan station with a hybrid livery combination of two blue and grey, and two maroon BR MK1 coaches comprising the afternoon service from Mallaig to Fort William in August 1968.

Alan Carlaw

#182 BRCW Type 2 Bo-Bo D.E. #D5358 comes off the speed restricted world renowned massed arch curved concrete viaduct at Glenfinnan with a short train from Fort William to Mallaig on a gloomy day in June 1962.

Roy M.B. Crombie/SRPS

#183 Blue liveried NBL Type 2 Bo-Bo D.E. #D6107 enters Tyndrum Upper station with a Mallaig to Glasgow service on the 8th June 1968. Note the ex LNER passenger brake van between the Locomotive and the Buffet car.

Hamish Stevenson

#184 Weathered, grimy and 'rust-runny' BRCW Type 2 Bo-Bo D.E. #D5348 arrives at Garelochhead station with a service from Fort William to Glasgow Queen Street on a hot and hazy 8th June 1965. *Robin Nelson*

#185 BRCW Type 2 Bo-Bo D.E. #27020 crosses the River Leven at Dumbarton with a Glasgow Queen Street to Fort William service on 27th March 1980. Note the ubiquitous west of Scotland tenements facing onto the railway. *Geo. C. O'Hara*

#186 Unidentified BRCW Type 2 Bo-Bo D.E. storms past the island platform station at Dumbarton East with an Oban to Glasgow service on 11th March 1980. On the level ground to left and beyond the station was sited the former LMSR Dumbarton locomotive (sub) shed. *Geo. C. O'Hara*

#187 BRCW Type 2 Bo-Bo D.E. #D5358 and a two coach train for Connel Ferry at Ballachullish during May 1964, when the goods service on the branch was still operating, as evinced by the vanfit and open wagon in one of the yard sidings adjacent to the wooden built goods shed. To the left of the goods shed were a spread of sidings where alumina traffic was unloaded from presflo wagons into road tankers for the short journey to the nearby Kinlochleven smelter of the British Aluminium Co. Ltd. This traffic ceased in 1965. *G.N.Turnbull*

#188 BRCW Type 2 Bo-Bo D.E. #D5365 at Appin with a service from Connel Ferry to Ballachullish on 18th September 1965. Just north of this station the line ran alongside the Sound of Shuna, and Loch Linnhe. From carriage windows excellent views of the mountains of Morvern and Ardgour could be seen, along with the iconic Castle Stalker built on an islet not far from the shore, and within sight of Appin station. *Roy Hamilton*

#189 EE Type 3 Co-Co D.E. #37022 and sister locomotive #37051 at Oban on 14th March 1983. The former engine, leaking steam is shunting empty coaching stock towards the station. and the latter has in tow a rake of empty oil tanks, bound for Mossend Yard and Grangemouth refinery of British Petroleum Ltd. *Tom H. Noble*

#190 Imposing view of EE Type 3 Co-Co D.E. #37033 thundering through glacial Glen Lochy with an Oban to Glasgow Queen Street service made up of BR Mk1 coaches in blue and grey livery on 30th April 1984. *Tom H. Noble*

#191 NBL Type 2 Bo-Bo D.E. #D6109 and #D6110 prepare tc restart the evening Oban to Glasgov Buchanan Street service away fron Crianlarich Lower on the rain and mis shrouded 17th June 1961. Note the ex LMSR sleeping coach behind the secon (train) locomotive. *WAC Smith/TT*

#192 Unidentified BRCW Type 2 Bo Bo D.E. hauls an Oban to Glasgov Buchanan Street service past the tin Loch Iubhair at the head of Gle Dochart on a wet day in March 1963. *Roy M.B. Crombie/SRPS*

#193 A pair of BRCW Type 2 Bo-Bo DE.'s #D5362 and #D5348 make light work of a lengthy Oban to Glasgow Buchanan Street and Edinburgh Princes Street combined train on the wet and misty Glen Dochart side of Glenoglehead on 2nd July 1965. *Michael Mensing*

#194 BRCW Type 2 Bo-Bo D.E. #D5360 descends Glenogle with an excursion run for Glasgow University in June 1963. Note the steady gradient of the A85 road on the east side of the glen. This four mile climb is a road 'feared and favoured' by Scotland's racing cyclists! *Roy M.B. Crombie/SRPS*

#195 Unidentified BRCW Type 2 Bo-Bo D.E. growls symphonically over one of the many curved viaducts as it toils up Glenogle with an eight coach Glasgow Buchanan Street to Oban service in May 1964, just over one year before this very scenic and under-valued railway line was closed prematurely due to a rock fall on 27th September 1965. *G.N. Turnbull*

#196 The spectacular glacial valley of Glenogle is seen to good effect as a pair of the stylish, but unreliable NBL Type 2 Bo-Bo D.E.s #D6102 and #D6123 make an exhaust free climb to the summit with the lightly loaded combined Edinburgh Princes Street and Glasgow Buchanan Street service to Oban on 17th May 1961. *Michael Mensing*

#197 Just above the village of Lochearnhead, a pair of NBL Type 2 Bo-Bo's #D6108 and #D6135 start the six mile climb from Balquihidder to Glenoglehead with the combined Edinburgh Princes Street and Glasgow Buchanan Street to Oban service on 13th May 1961. *Michael Mensing*

#198 The crew of NBL Type 2 Bo-Bo D.E. #D6130 and #D6123 double headed locomotive combination in charge of a service from Glasgow Buchanan Street to Oban top up the train heating boiler of the lead engine from the ex CR water crane at the north end of Balquihidder on 3rd April 1961. *Hamish Stevenson*

#199 NBL Type 2 Bo-Bo D.E.s #D6120 and #D6129 skirt the west side of Loch Lubnaig south of Strathyre with a lightweight four coach Glasgow Buchanan Street to Oban train on 12th August 1961. Behind the rear of the train can be seen the east flanks of Ben Vane (2685ft). *WAC Smith/TTT*

#200 Unidentified NBL Type 2 Bo-Bo DE. makes a caliginous emission of engine exhaust gases as it leaves Kirkintilloch with an empty coaching stock working during August 1963. In the distance the mist shrouded outline of the Kilsyth Hills can just be seen. *WAC Smith/TTT*

#201 NBL Type 2 Bo-Bo D.E. #D6110 near Middlemuir Junction Lenzie, with a service from Glasgow Queen Street to Kirkintilloch on 6th August 1963. *Douglas Hume*

#202 NBL Type 2 Bo-Bo #D6105 passes Whifflet Lower yard with a service from Coatbridge Central to Holytown on 21st September 1962. In the train consist is an ex LMSR two coach articulated suburban set. On either side of the main line are rakes of plate and tube wagons, timely reminders of the once inter-linked dependency of British Railways and the former steel making industry of Lanarkshire. *Roy Hamilton*

#203 BRCW Type 2 Bo-Bo D.E. #26025 (running-in after an ex-works overhaul) pilots Brush Type 4 Co-Co D.E. #47040 on a Glasgow Queen Street to Perth service past the east end of Cadder Yard on the 18th January 1983. *Tom H. Noble*

#204 Part of the skyline of the City of Glasgow can be seen as EE Type 4 1Co-Co1 D.E. #40064 climbs Cowlairs Bank with a Glasgow Queen Street to Aberdeen train on 6th August 1981. *Tom H. Noble*

#205 NBL Type 2 Bo-Bo D.E.s #D6113 and #D6137 arrive at Glasgow Buchanan Street with a service from Dundee West on 18th February 1961, where on an adjacent platform an unidentified ex LNER V2 2-6-2 locomotive is at the head of a northbound working. *WAC Smith/TTT*

#206 BRCW Type 2 Bo-Bo D.E. #D5349 passes Possilpark with the afternoon Glasgow Queen Street to Mallaig service on 10th September 1963. Note the unidentified EE Type 1 Bo-Bo D.E. and brake van in the adjacent and overgrown goods yard, and the short branch to Ruchill Goods Yard trailing off to the right.
WAC Smith/TTT

#207 An autumnal evening sky compliments the rooftops of the Kelvindale suburb of Glasgow as Clayton Type 1 Bo-Bo D.E. #D8525 crosses the substantial River Kelvin stone and steel viaduct between Bellshaugh Junction and Kelvinside Junction with a Rutherglen to Possil service on 10th September 1963.
WAC Smith/TTT

#208 EE Type 4 1Co-Co1 D.E. #40064 passes the former National Coal Board Cardowan Colliery at Stepps with a diverted Glasgow Queen Street to Aberdeen service on 22nd July 1979.

Morrison Bryce

#209 EE Type 4 Co-Co D.E. #50017 throbs purposefully at Glasgow Central before taking out a southbound express in the summer of 1974.

WAC Smith/TTT

#210 EE Type 4 Co-Co D.E. #50022 lays a viscous trail of engine exhaust in its wake as it storms past Strathbungo with a diverted southbound express on 3rd July 1974.

WAC Smith/TTT

#211 NBL Type 2 Bo-Bo D.E. #D6122 rattles a lengthy football special from Hampden Park (Mount Florida Station) back to Glasgow Central near Maxwell Park, in April 1969. This locomotive remained stored at the Dia Woodham scrapyard in Barry, South Wales for many years after it had been withdrawn by British Railways, but alas it did not escape the cutter's torch, and was thus lost for preservation.

Jack Kernahan

#212 The cranes of the former Lithgow Group Kingston, Glen and East shipbuilding yards combine with the array of different types of tenements and prefabs to illustrate the landscape of once industrial Port Glasgow, as Clayton Type 1 Bo-Bo D.E. #D8508 rattles a service from Glasgow Central to Gourock past Ladyburn signal box on 6th July 1963. *WAC Smith/TTT*

#213 BR Type 4 1Co-Co1 D.E. #D11 powers up the Neilston bank alongside the A736 with a service from Glasgow St. Enoch to Leeds on the 14th July 1961.

WAC Smith/TTT

#214 EE Type 3 Co-Co D.E. #37246 rattles a five coach rake of BR Mk 1 coaches in the gaudy Sealink mock ice cream van livery, past Howwood signal box with a service from Glasgow Central to Stranraer on 12th July 1984.

Tom H. Noble

#215 Unidentified EE Type 1 Bo-Bo passes the former C.R. Ardrossan North Station en route to nearby Montgomerie Pier with a boat train in July 1964. Note the bogie well wagons loaded with steel plates in trestles bound for the Harland & Wolff Ltd., shipyard in Belfast, many 4-wheel Shell bitumen tank wagons, and the hawker pulling his barrow.

Roy M.B. Crombie/SRPS

#216 The driver of unidentified smoke begrimed ex-LMS Crab 2-6-0 exudes some of the aura that proclaims "The sureness of steam" as his locomotive renders tender first pilot assistance to a failed unidentified Brush Type 4 Co-Co D.E. in charge of a school excursion to a destination in Ayrshire south of Lochgreen Junction in July 1965.

WAC Smith/TTT

#217 Unidentified Brush Type 4 Co-Co D.E. powers past Ayr loco shed with a service from Stranraer to Euston via the GSWR line on 9th April 1982.

Geo. C. O'Hara

#218 BRCW Type 2 Bo-Bo D.E. #D5369 leaves the former station of Heads of Ayr, which served the adjacent Butlins Holiday Camp with a service to Newcastle on the hot and hazy 24th August 1968.

Douglas Hume

#219 Unidentified EE Type 4 1Co-Co1 D.E. whistles and thunders over the infant River Clyde at what has become known as "Derek Cross's bridge" between Crawford and Abington with a lengthy northbound express from England in the 1960's. *Jack Kernahan*

#220 The conical cusp of one of the south Lanarkshire Laws provides the backdrop to EE Type 4 1Co-Co1 D.E. #D339 powering through Abington station with a southbound express from Glasgow Central on 4th June 1962. *Robin Nelson*

#221 EE Type 4 1Co-Co1 D.E. #D344 clatters past Beattock South signal box with a service from Birmingham New Street to Edinburgh Princes Street on 4th August 1962, as ex-LMSR Fairburn 2-6-4 tank #42693 awaits its next banking duty. *WAC Smith/TTT*

#222 BRCW Type 2 Bo-Bo D.E. #D5355 heads a Glasgow Central to Carlisle stopping service north of Abington sometime in the 1960's. *Jack Kernahan*

#223 BR Type 4 1Co-Co1 D.E. #D117 leaves Thankerton station with a Glasgow Central to Carlisle stopping service in the summer of 1963. *WAC Smith/TTT*

#224 BRCW Type 2 Bo-Bo D.E. #D5303 burbles past Lady Victoria Colliery at Newtongrange with the mid-day Edinburgh Waverley to Carlisle stopping service over the former Waverley route on 30th December 1961.
Douglas Hume

#225 BRCW Type 2 Bo-Bo D.E. #D5301 crosses over the infant Gala Water near the village of Stow with an Edinburgh Waverley to Hawick service on 7th February 1965.
Douglas Hume

#226 Unidentified BRCW Type 2 Bo-Bo D.E. descend Falahill Bank on 3rd Augus 1968 with a lightweigh Carlisle to Edinburg Waverley stopping trai comprising four vehicle including two bogie parce vans. *G.N. Turnbu*

#227 Unidentified BRCW Type 2 Bo-Bo D.E. between Stow and Galashiels with an Edinburgh Waverley to Carlisle stopping service on 17th August 1968.
G.N. Turnbull

#228 Unidentified BR Type 4 1Co-Co1 D.E. south of St Boswells with an Up Waverley route express in July 1966.
Roy M.B. Crombie/SRPS

#229 Unidentified BR Type 4 1Co-Co1 D.E. still resplendent in original British Railways Brunswick green livery leaves Bowshank Tunnel on 3rd August 1968 with a down Waverley route express. *G.N. Turnbull*

#230 Unidentified BRCW Type 2 Bo-Bo D.E. rolls into the isolated station at Riccarton Junction with an Edinburgh Waverley to Carlisle stopping service in August 1966. *Roy M.B. Crombie/SRPS*

Section 5

STATIONS

At the formation of British Railways in 1948 there were approximately 1000 passenger stations within the acquired inventory of real estate vested in the semi-autonomous Scottish Region. Most of these stations had been built by the initial railway developer companies, and became the property of each successive consolidation of the British railway network. They ranged from the few multiple platform cast-iron, steel, concrete and glass edifices built in Glasgow and Edinburgh to the many, sometimes unstaffed, wayside halts scattered throughout Scotland. There were also several commodious but less grand stations in the many provincial towns and cities, as well as at some busy junctions, and a plethora of suburban locations.

Most of these stations remained basically unaltered throughout the era that was British Railways, save for occasional repaints and modernisation works necessary for subsequent electrification and signalling upgrades on selected routes. Publication of "The reshaping of British Railways" report in 1963 led very quickly to a decade of closure, and austere rationalisation of stations. Many hundreds of stations were closed, or reduced in status to that of unmanned, whence they were vandalised, before being ultimately replaced by a bus shelter made of toughened glass.

The collection of photographs in this section attempts to depict railway activity at several different examples of the diverse spectrum of stations that was the hallmark of the Scottish Region of British Railways, during the time when all of the types of new diesel traction were being introduced.

LIST OF LOCATIONS ILLUSTRATED

#231 The frugal station at WICK barely covers the two coach portion of a service to Inverness hauled by BRCW Type 2 Bo-Bo D.E. #D5343 in the mid-1960's. This train will be lengthened at Georgemas Junction with the additional of several coaches from Thurso. *Ken Nuttall*

#232 A misty east coast of Scotland harr shrouds the background as BRCW Type 2 Bo-Bo D.E. #D5342 stops at SCOTSCALDER with an 'up' passenger service in the mid-1960's. *Ken Nuttall*

#233 Probably the first visit to the far north line of an EE Type 1 Bo-Bo D.E. on a passenger train occurred on 16th April 1960 when #D8032 deputised for a failed ex-LMS Class 5 4-6-0 on a soutbound working at DINGWALL. *Douglas Hume*

#234 The unique and very Scottish railway station at KYLE OF LOCHALSH is teeming with freight traffic in the form of vans and tank wagons as an unidentified BRCW Type 2 Bo-Bo D.E. prepares to depart with a four coach train for Inverness on 17th August 1972. *G.N.Turnbull*

#235 The former HR station at STROMEFERRY on Loch Carron was quickly converted into a rail/ship transfer facility in the early 1970's to minimise the impact on the adjacent roads, as the nearby Howard-Doris concrete offshore platform construction yard was initiated, and materials were transferred there by British Railways. The yard barely lasted ten years, and rail traffic never met the volumes anticipated. On 16th June 1982 a pair of BRCW Type 2 Bo-Bo D.E.s #26035 and #26042 leave the station with a Kyle of Lochalsh to Inverness service. *Tom H. Noble*

#236 The quaint and substantial station and hotel buildings at ACHNASHEEN provide the backdrop to BRCW Type 2 Bo-Bo D.E. #5333 (by now minus its D prefix), as it restarts a Kyle of Lochalsh to Inverness service on 29th June 1973. *Ken Falconer*

#237 INVERNESS station is approached by a three car BR Swindon DMU from Aberdeen, and is about to be left by a service to Glasgow and Edinburgh piloted by BRCW Type 2 Bo-Bo D.E. #26041 during the late 1970s.

Jack Kernahan

#238 The unique triangular station at FORRES is about to be departed by a lengthy southbound passenger service over the former HR main line via Dava Summit on 13th August 1960. Piloting a former LMS Class 5 4-6-0 #45492 is a very new looking BRCW Type 2 Bo-Bo D.E. #D5331, as the pair pass the austere signal cabin to the south of the station.

Douglas Hume

#239 The open and windswept former HR station at DAVA is passed by a pair of unidentified BRCW Type 2 D.E.s hauling a northbound goods, and a southbound passenger service during June 1965. Note the returning empty whisky casks in two 13 ton open wagons.

Roy M.B. Crombie/SRPS

#240 An unidentified BRCW Type 2 Bo-Bo D.E. crawls away from the austere station at DUNPHAIL on the former HR main line with the morning service from Inverness to Aviemore on 27th August 1965, a few weeks before withdrawal of passenger services on the line. *Roy Hamilton*

#241 The former GNSR station at GRANTOWN ON SPEY EAST is about to be departed by one of the stylish but shooglie, under-powered and noisy Park Royal 4-wheel diesel railbuses on 16th June 1962. Notable in the photograph is a long rake of fitted vans stored in the goods yard, and underneath the footbridge on the opposite station platform can be seen the late Roy Hamilton, MBE., career railwayman and eminent railway photographer and historian. *Douglas Hume*

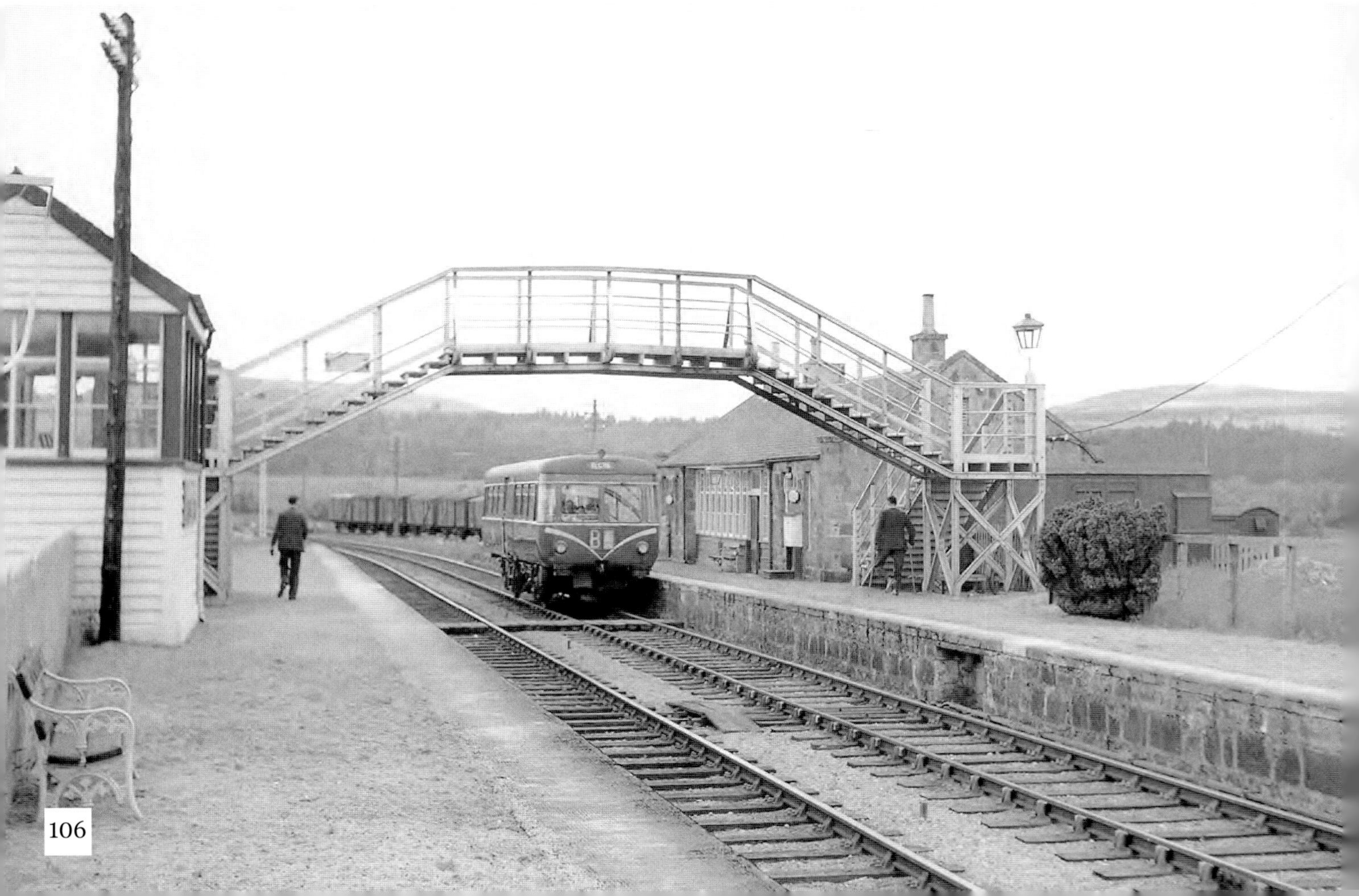

#242 ABERLOUR on the former GNSR Speyside line is visited by BR 0-6-0 350 h.p. D.E. shunter #15229 as it passes through with a diesel hauled test train from Keith to Boat of Garten on 29th October 1958. *Roy Hamilton*

#243 The bay platform of ELGIN is occupied by NBL Type 2 Bo-Bo D.E. #D6143 leaking steam from its train heating system, as it awaits to depart with a two coach service to Lossiemouth during March 1963. *Norris Forrest/TTT*

#244 Three different trains can be seen at four of the former GNSR Coast and Glen route platforms at ELGIN in October 1967, seven months before closure of both of these routes. *G.N.Turnbull*

#245 The former GNSR station of LOSSIEMOUTH is departed by a mixed train for Elgin hauled by NBL Type 2 Bo-Bo D.E. #D6141 on the last day of passenger services on the branch, 4th April 1964. Note the posse of small boys waving to the driver and passengers of the departing service. *Roy Hamilton*

#246 KINTORE was the former junction station for the Alford branch, seen veering off to the left. In June 1960 it was visited by a railtour, the five coaches of which can be seen to the left. Also on view are an unidentified NBL Type 2 Bo-Bo D.E. held in the loop beyond the station, awaiting the passing of a westbound train. On the platform to the extreme left is WAC (Bill) Smith, and wearing the kilt, near the platform edge is Norris Forrest, both eminent railway photographers and historians of note, and sadly both since deceased. *Roy Hamilton*

#247 NBL Type 2 Bo-Bo D.E. #D6151 stops at CORNHILL in Banffshire with an Elgin to Aberdeen via the Coast line service on 20th June 1964, when the nearby goods yard was still operational. *Roy Hamilton*

#248 Cravens 2-car DMU decants passengers at the wayside station of CAIRNBULG en route to St. Combs from Fraserburgh on 16th June 1960. *Roy Hamilton*

#249 Looking more like a school playground shelter than a railway station, the austere and unpatronised station at MINTLAW is about to be visited by a Peterhead to Maud Junction (and Aberdeen) service hauled by NBL Type 2 Bo-Bo D.E. #D6140 on 24th April 1965, a few weeks before passenger services were withdrawn from the branch. *Jack Kernahan*

#250 The soon to be closed station at FRASERBURGH is being visited by (rarely seen on the Buchan Line during passenger services), BRCW Type 2 Bo-Bo D.E. #D5347 with a four coach service for Aberdeen on 2nd October 1965.
Roy Hamilton

#251 MAUD JUNCTION station on 21st September 1963 with NBL Type 2 Bo-Bo D.E. #D6139 on a two coach train for Peterhead. Note the water tower and filling bag at the end of the platform. *Douglas Hume*

#252 A plethora of fitted vanfits depicts a symmetry of burgeoning freight traffic at PETERHEAD, as NBL Type 2 Bo-Bo DE. #D6140 waits at the head of a two coach service to Maud Junction on 27th March 1963. *Robin Nelson*

#253 The turretted witches' hat embellishments of ABOYNE station are seen to good effect as an evening service from Ballater to Aberdeen stops for passengers on 11th May 1960. *Roy Hamilton*

#254 Re-engined and re-painted in two tone green livery NBL Type 2 Bo-Bo D.E. #D6106 stops at FORFAR with a northbound service for Aberdeen during August 1967, a month before withdrawal of passenger train services from the Angus town. *Norris Forrest/TTT*

#255 Unidentified BRCW Type 2 Bo-Bo D.E. takes the Speyside Line at Aviemore with a northbound service for Inverness via Dava and Forres during the Autumn of 1964.
Ken Nuttall

#256 Hybrid double heading of BR Type 2, and BRCW Type 2 Bo-Bo D.E. #D5112 and #D5326 enter the wayside station at STRUAN with an Inverness to Glasgow Buchanan Street working on 3rd April 1965.
Roy Hamilton

#257 A pair of unidentified BR Type 2 Bo-Bo D.E.s enter PITLOCHRY, where the automatic tablet catching apparatus can be seen between the goods shed and the station platform in front of the leading locomotive, hauling a lengthy Inverness to Glasgow and Edinburgh train during the summer of 1963. Note the still operational goods sidings on both the 'Up' and 'Down' lines.
WAC Smith/TTT

#258 The former HR station at DUNKELD & BIRNAM is still in possession of a water crane, and the last gaslit lighting in Scotland as BRCW Type 2 Bo-Bo D.E. #D5334 awaits the passing of a northbound service on 3rd April 1965. *Jack Kernahan*

#259 The station building at KINROSS JUNCTION were a very typical edifice as built in Scotland by the former NBR. On 13th December 1969, shortly before total closure of the line through Glenfarg, BRCW Type 2 Bo-Bo D.E.s #D5344 and #D5339 pass the station junction signal box with a service from Inverness to Edinburgh Waverley. *Douglas Hume*

#260 Unidentified BRCW Type 2 Bo-Bo D.E. stops at the wayside station of Glenfarg with a Perth to Edinburgh Waverley service on 28th March 1966. *Robin Nelson*

#261 SHANDON station on the Gare Loch was a typical island platform structure which was replicated throughout the West Highland Line. On 25th January 1964 BRCW Type 2 Bo-Bo D.E. #D5331 awaits the arrival of a southbound working, before heading north with the 11.25 Yoker Yard to Fort William goods working. Note the six empty Blue Spot insul fish vans in the consist, being returned to Mallaig. *Douglas Hume*

#262 The wayside halt of WHISTLEFIELD looks decidedly more European than Scottish, with its steep roof, ornate chimney pots and fancy finials. A Park Royal 4-wheel diesel railbus decants a single passenger as the guard telephones ahead before the service from Craigendoran departs for Arrochar and Tarbet on 25th January 1964. *Douglas Hume*

PREVIOUS PAGE:
#263 The island platform of ARROCHAR and TARBET is the scene of the passing of northbound and southbound trains to/from Oban on 8th June 1968. NBL Type 2 Bo-Bo D.E. #D6132 is in charge of the southbound service, and sister locomotive #D6123 is in charge of the northbound working. *Hamish Stevenson*

#264 The original NB station at FORT WILLIAM, part of the pier, and a few buses belonging to the David MacBrayne company are seen in this view of 11th August, 1965, as BRCW Type 2 Bo-Bo D.E. #D5365 prepares to leave with a service for Glasgow Queen Street. *Ken Falconer*

#265 Repainted in BR Rail blue livery and devoid of its D prefix, NBL Type 2 Bo-Bo D.E.#6119 idles at the still partly covered MALLAIG station before working a service to Fort William in March 1969. *Norris Forrest/TTT*

#266 MALLAIG nearly twenty years later on 28th July 1988 sees large logo adorned EE Type 3 Co-Co D.E. #37406 "The Sattire Society" propelling stock towards the station. Note how recent road improvements have consumed most of the former steam shed area, and the last remaining freight to the station is fuel oil delivered to the siding on the right. *Tom H. Noble*

#267 BALLACHULISH in March 1966, shortly before the total closure of the branch with an unidentified BRCW Type 2 Bo-Bo D.E. at the head of a short rake of BR suburban coaches. Note the enthusiast photographing a scene which will soon be part of Scottish transport history. *Alan Carlaw*

#268 Unidentified BRCW Type 2 Bo-Bo D.E. splutters away from OBAN with a three coach service for Ballachulish during March 1965. Noticeable in this view are several Blue Spot insul fish vans, fuel oil tankers, and the once seemingly ubiquitous ferry tsmv Claymore, 1024g.r.t., moored alongside the quay. *WAC Smith/TTT*

#269 An evening scene of traction transition at OBAN on 22nd January 1989, sees EE Type 3 Co-Co D.E. #37408 "Loch Rannoch" in charge of the last booked loco-hauled passenger service from the station, before the advent of BR built Class 156 Sprinter DMUs the next day. *Tom H. Noble*

#270 BRCW Type 2 Bo-Bo D.E. #D5355 stops at the island platform station at CONNEL FERRY with a service for Glasgow Buchanan Street on 12th May 1962. Note the Presflo wagons in the right of this view used to convey alumina from the B.A. Co. Ltd., works at Burntisland to Ballachulish. This traffic ceased in 1965. *Douglas Hume*

#271 DUNDEE TAY BRIDGE on 23rd June 1960 with BRCW Type 2 Bo-Bo D.E. #D5305 and D5306 in charge of a service from Aberdeen to Edinburgh. *Ken Nuttall*

#272 A pair of Metro-Cammell 2-car DMUs are seen at LEUCHARS JUNCTION station on 3rd January 1969 in charge of local services to Dundee on the left and St. Andrews in the bay platforms respectively. *G.N.Turnbull*

#273 A well patronised Metro-Cammell 3-car DMU decants a considerable number of passengers at WORMIT station at the south side of the Tay Bridge, whilst working a serv ce from Dundee Tay Bridge to Tayport on 1st May 1965. The building to the left was later dismantled and re-erected as the Bo-ness station on the SRPS Bo'ness and Kinneil railway.
Roy Hamilton

#274 A 4-car hybrid DMU comprising a 2-car Cravens unit leading and a 2-car Metro-Cammell unit trailing are seen at NEWPORT-ON-TAY EAST with a Dundee Tay Bridge to Tayport service during May 1965. Note the covered coal depots of Messrs. Smith Hood & Co. Ltd., and Thos. Muir Son & Patton Ltd., in the still functional goods yard. This provision of weather protection for the men who shovelled empty the contents of each coal wagon, was quite common at several former Scottish coal merchants sidings.
Roy Hamilton

#275 The single platform station at GUARDBRIDGE on the truncated branch to St.Andrews is visited by Gloucester R.C & W. Co. 2-car DMU with a service to Leuchars Junction on 28th December 1968. *Douglas Hume*

#276 3-car Metro-Cammell DMU departs from PITTENWEEM with a service from St.Andrews to Edinburgh Waverley on 3rd October 1959. Note the open wagons loaded with what appears to be sugar beet alongside the high platform in the goods yard. *Douglas Hume*

#277 A busy holiday scene at LARGO station as a 6-car Metro-Cammell DMU decants several holidaymakers from a Glasgow Buchanan Street to Dundee Tay Bridge service, while ex-LNER B1 4-6-0 #61076 prepares to leave on a southbound service on 18th July 1962. *Douglas Hume*

#278 BRCW Type 2 Bo-Bo D.E. #D5329 at ABERFELDY with a two coach service for Ballinluig Junction on 27th July 1964. The former location of the station and goods yard was quickly sold off after the closure of the branch line, and the site was later occupied by many new houses. *Ken Falconer*

#279 The quaint and basic one platform station of GRANDTULLY is visited by BR Type 2 Bo-Bo D.E. #D5123 on a one-coach railbus 'equivalent' service from Ballinluig Junction to Aberfeldy on 3rd April 1965 shortly before the total closure of the branch. The goods service had already been withdrawn earlier that year. *Roy Hamilton*

PREVIOUS PAGE:

#280 Bristol/Eastern Coach Works 4-wheel diesel railbus at a seemingly deserted and rain soaked COMRIE on 31st August, 1963. Note the water tower and camping coach beyond the platform awning in the adjacent goods yard.
Douglas Hume

#281 The ornate station at CRIEFF looks far too over-sized to accommodate a Park Royal 4-wheel diesel railbus in June 1964, a month before the passenger service was withdrawn from the attractive Perthshire town.
Roy M.B. Crombie/SRPS

#282 The last day of service on the branch line to Crieff and Comrie sees Park Royal 4-wheel diesel railbus receive signal clearance at the junction station of GLENEAGLES on 4th July 1964. Note the extent of looped, interlocked and signal controlled trackwork at the junction station.This impressive railway infrastructure was soon removed after the last train had traversed the branch.
Roy Hamilton

#283 A terrific Scottish transitional railway scene at the architecturally unique CALLANDER station during April 1959, when the former British Railways were an essential element of the transport infrastructure of the country. From left to right a 4-wheel horse-box (probably of LMSR ancestry) waits in the bay platform to load one or more of the local Laird's mares or fillies. A Cravens DMU lets passengers alight from one of the then very popular "Six Lochs Land Cruises" which ran from Glasgow Buchanan Street in the summer months. Two former LMS Class 5 4-6-0 locomotives #45153 and #45213 prepare to depart for Glasgow with passenger and goods trains from Oban respectively. *WAC Smith/TTT*

#284 CALLANDER station prior to its closure on a wet 30th October 1965 sees a hybrid 4-car DMU led by a 2-car Metro-Cammell unit leading a Gloucester R.C. & W. pair splutter away from the station with the peak of Ben Ledi (2882ft.) prominent despite the pervasive Scotch mist surrounding the summit. *Douglas Hume*

#285 The same service as depicted in the previous view is seen arriving at DOUNE, with its unique covered footbridge, on the last day of service on the line. Recent increases in the population of this town, and the growing popularity of Callander as a tourist centre, question the folly in the closure and dismantling of this line, the trackbed of which is still intact except for road re-alignments and the development of both former station sites. *David C. Smith*

#286 D. Wickham 4-wheel diesel railbus at one of the bay platforms at the north end of STIRLING station with an evening service for Alloa on 21st November 1961. *Ken Falconer*

#287 Most of the through and some of the bay platforms at the north end of STIRLING station can be seen on 9th June 1989 as EE Type 3 Co-Co D.E. #37063 trundles through with a lengthy rake of molasses tanks and Polybulk grain wagons bound for Menstrie and Cambus respectively. *Tom H. Noble*

NEXT PAGE:
#288 A bundle of parcels is unloaded by the guard of a Stirling to Dollar service in the charge of a Metro-Cammell 2-car DMU at TILLICOULTRY station on the Devon Valley Line on 23rd May 1964. *Douglas Hume*

#289 LARBERT station on 29th August 1966 with a Cravens 2-car DMU in the bay platform bound for Edinburgh Waverley, and an unidentified BRCW Type 2 Bo-Bo D.E. in charge of a southbound stopping train. *Roy Hamilton*

#290 Metro-Cammell 3-car DMU accentuates the autumnal evening shadows at KIRKINTILLOCH on 1st September 1964 with a return service to Glasgow Queen Street, shortly before the passenger service was withdrawn on the branch, which used to extend to Aberfoyle and Kilsyth. *Roy Hamilton*

2B

EDINBURGH

3K
10

#291 CLYDEBANK RIVERSIDE station shortly before closure and withdrawal of passenger train services on 2nd October 1964, is seen with Cravens 2-car DMU about to leave on an eastbound service. An unidentified 2-6-4 tank locomotive passes on the other line bound for Dalmuir Riverside. This station was used by workers from the nearby world famous shipyard of John Brown & Co. (Clydebank) Ltd. *Roy Hamilton*

#292 SPRINGBURN station on a scorching 17th June 1978 before the installation of the Cowlairs curve allowed through running from Glasgow Queen Street to Cumbernauld. Passengers change trains between a re-liveried Metro-Cammell 3-car DMU and a north-bank Class 311 EMU on adjacent platforms. *Tom H. Noble*

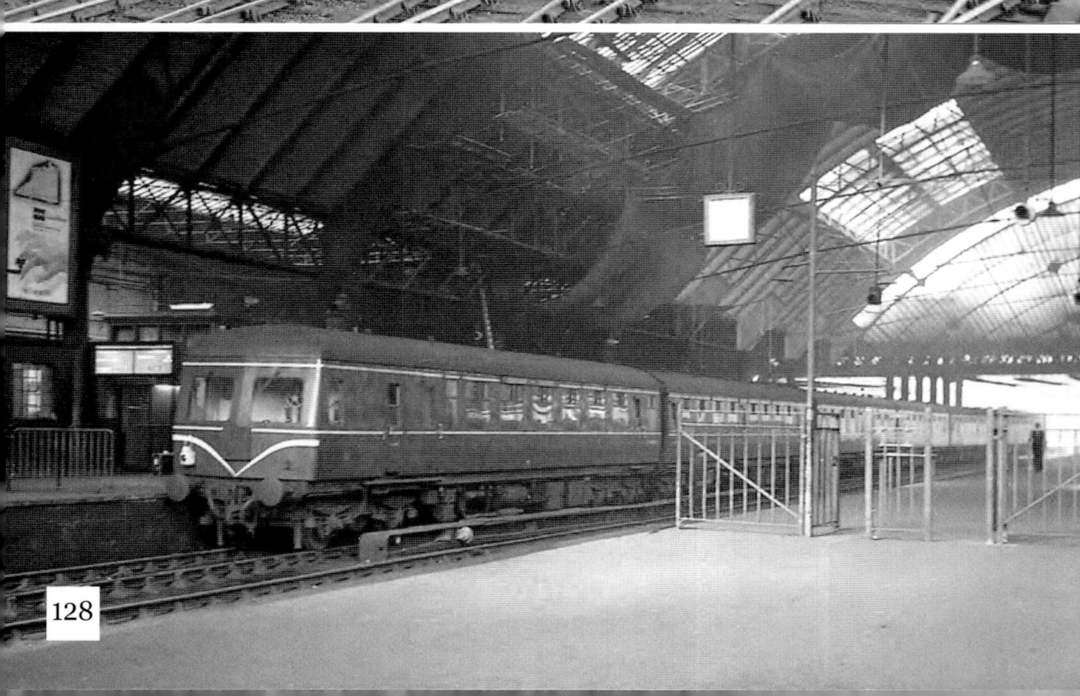

#293 GLASGOW BUCHANAN STREET in the mid-1960's when ex-LNER A4 pacific class locos replaced the errant NBL Type 2's on the 3 hour services to Aberdeen. One such working is seen departing from the station headed by #60007 "Sir Nigel Gresley" as an unidentified BRCW Type 2 Bo-Bo D.E. waits with a service on the adjacent platform.
WAC Smith/TT

#294 EE Type 4 1Co-Co1 D.E #D334 leaves GLASGOW BUCHANAN STREET station with the regular Sunday up postal train on 28th May 1961, when the adjoining goods station was still open. *WAC Smith/TT*

STA#295 GLASGOW QUEEN STREET station in June 1960 is still an almost cavernous soot begrimed glass and steel arch-roofed edifice from the steam era, as BR Swindon 6 car DMU prepares with a service to Edinburgh Waverley.
Roy M.B. Crombie/SRP

#296 Still in original BR green livery but with full size yellow ends, and minus its D prefix, EE Type 4 1Co-Co1 D.E. #357 leaves the deep excavated cutting of GLASGOW QUEEN STREET station with a service for Aberdeen on the 4th September 1971.
Jack Kernahan

#297 Metro-Cammell 3-car DMU brings a service from Edinburgh Princes Street into GLASGOW CENTRAL station over the former Caledonian Railway birdcage bridge over the River Clyde on 23rd January 1960. *WAC Smith/TTT*

#298 At the head of trains in adjacent platforms, the locomotive crews of BR Std. Class 5 4-6-0 #73072 and unidentified Brush Type 4 Co-Co D.E. indulge in a "relief of steam" contest at GLASGOW CENTRAL station in the spring of 1965. *WAC Smith/TTT*

#**299** The slab sided bulk of EE Type 4 Co-Co D.E. #50046 is shown to good effect as it hums into GLASGOW CENTRAL station with an express service from England in July 1974. *WAC Smith/TTT*

#**300** Unidentified BR Type 4 1Co-Co1 D.E. at GLASGOW ST. ENOCH with the IM 86 the famous "Thames-Clyde" express service to England, as an unidentified ex-LMS Class 5 4-6-0 runs out tender first with a local suburban service sometime in the early 1960s. *WAC Smith/TTT*

#**301** Most of both of the impressive two steel and glass arches of the former GLASGOW ST ENOCH station can be seen as BR Swindon DMU leaves with a service for Ayr in March 1966. Note the rake of 4-wheel vans used for parcels traffic, and the bonnet of an unidentified Clayton Type 1 Bo-Bo D.E. *WAC Smith/TTT*

#302 Clayton Type I Bo-Bo D.E. #D8529 at KILBARCHAN station with one of the last passenger services on the former Brownhill Junction – Kilbirnie – Elderslie Line on 11th June 1966. The wooden white painted building in the foreground housed the stairway leading from the station platform to the street below. *Hamish Stevenson*

#303 Hybrid 4-car DMU comprising of Gloucester R. C. & W. Co. 2-car leading and Cravens 2-car DMU trailing, stops at RENFREW SOUTH station during July 1967, a few weeks before withdrawal of passenger train services on the short branch to Renfrew Wharf from Arkleston Junction.
Jack Kernahan

#304 Smoke begrimed BR Std. Class 5 4-6-0 #73059 heads towards the turntable at Gourock, as unidentified NBL 0-4-0 225 hp. D.H. shunter moves a rake of BR suburban coaches towards GOUROCK station in July 1966. *WAC Smith/TTT*

#305 GOUROCK station, yard, pier and quayside in a pouring wet misty West of Scotland day, during March 1964. An unidentified EE 0-6-0 350 h.p. D.E. shunter can be seen near the signal box.
Norris Forrest/TTT

#306 BR Type 2 Bo-Bo D.E. #D7595 passes through SHIELDS ROAD station with a service from Wemyss Bay to Glasgow Central on 10th October 1964.
Robin Nelson

#307 NBL Type 2 Bo-Bo D.E. #D6122 clatters through SHAWLANDS station with a football special to Mount Florida (for Hampden Park) in May 1966.
Jack Kernahan

#308 Gloucester R.C. & W. Co. 2-car DMU at the curved platforms of BRIDGETON CROSS junction station with a Rutherglen to Dalmuir Riverside service on 30th September 1964. This location and the line from Stobcross to Rutherglen was later re-instated and electrified by British Railways in 1979. The former line to Tollcross via Parkhead was unfortunately not included in this scheme, even with the inclusion of a new spur southwards adjoining the London Road branch. *Robin Nelson*

#309 BR Swindon 6-car DMU makes an exhaust plume of steam locomotive proportions as it leaves AYR station with a service for Glasgow Central on 11th April 1982. The imposing building behind is the town's iconic Station Hotel which has endured several different owners in its century of existence. *Geo. C. O'Hara*

#310 Park Royal 4-wheel diesel railbus complete with portable step at DALMELLINGTON with a service for AYR on 15th June 1963, when the unreliability of these units often led to their substitution by BR Standard Class 3 and 4 locomotives hauling two coach formations. *Douglas Hume*

#311 BR Type 4 1Co-Co1 DE. #D24 rumbles into LUGTON station, juction for the short branch line to Beith and Giffen, with a Glasgow St. Enoch to Carlisle stopping service on 22nd June 1961. *Robin Nelson*

#312 The neat and tidy former BEITH TOWN station built on a gentle concave arc plays host to A.C. Cars 4-wheel diesel railbus on 20th May 1960.

John N. Faulkner

#313 BR Derby 3-car DMU is seen in the single platform station at COALBURN during July 1964, where the architecture and ironmongery of the former age of steam are still functioning, and vandal free. The track in the foreground led to Auchlochan Colliery at Bankend. Coal traffic from this Lanarkshire pit kept this line open until 1968, some three years after the passenger service was withdrawn.

Roy M.B. Crombie/SRPS

#314 The large expanse of HAMILTON CENTRAL station is seen to good effect on the 16th August 1969, after track rationalisation has removed the former two centre roads which were no longer required following the wholesale contraction of the Lanarkshire coal mining industry. Parcels traffic is still however being uplifted. *WAC Smith/TTT*

#315 LANARK station on 20th March 1963 with BR Swindon and BR Derby 3-car DMUs on services to Glasgow and Muirkirk respectively.
Robin Nelson

#316 Two passengers prepare to board a Metro-Cammell 2-car DMU as it stops at PONFEIGH station with a service from Lanark to Muirkirk on 3rd August 1963. This village housed many miners who worked at the nearby Douglas colliery.
Hamish Stevenson

NEXT PAGE:
#317 The impressive former edifice that was EDINBURGH PRINCES STREET station on 4th September 1965 where an unidentified Clayton Type 1 Bo-Bo D.E. is seen backing onto to a service for Lanark. *Robin Nelson*

#318 The west end of EDINBURGH WAVERLEY station on 8th September 1986 with Brush Type 4 Co-Co D.E. #47709 "The Lord Provost" repainted in chic ScotRail livery about to leave with a "push-pull" service to Glasgow Queen Street. Unidentified EE Type 3 Co-Co D.E. and BRCW Type 2 Bo-Bo D.E. are seen to the right on services to Manchester and Dundee respectively. *Tom H. Noble*

EDINBURGH
PRINCES STREET

47 709
ScotRail

#319 The east end of EDINBURGH WAVERLEY station is shrouded in the engine exhaust of EE Deltic Type 5 Co-Co D.E. #D9014 "The Duke of Wellington's Regiment" as it leaves with a southbound express on 15th June 1964.
W.S. Sellar

#320 Unidentified BRCW Type 2 Bo-Bo D.E. arrives at GOREBRIDGE with an afternoon stopping service from Edinburgh Waverley to Hawick on 11th May 1963. Note the still operational goods yard served by a quaint reverse curve siding containing a single vanfit, and protected by a loading gauge. *WAC Smith/TTT*

#321 Gloucester R.C. & W. Co. 2-car DMU leaves MUSSELBURGH station and adjoining goods depot, crossing over the River Esk with a service for Edinburgh Waverley in June 1963. *WAC Smith/TTT*

#322 Gloucester R.C. & W. Co. 2-car DMU arrives at NORTH BERWICK station with its still very busy goods yard on a service from Corstorphine in May 1962. Note the pair of Camping Coaches in the right hand side of the extensive goods yard. In the left foreground is the dilapidated roof of the former locomotive shed. *WAC Smith/TTT*

#323 Gloucester R.C. & W. Co. 2-car DMU arrives at INNERLEITHEN, where the impressive station master's house is larger than the station buildings, with an Edinburgh Waverley to Galashiels via Peebles service on 18th November 1961. *WAC Smith/TTT*

#324 PEEBLES (ex N.B.) station is nicely framed by a footbridge, signal post and water crane, as Gloucester R.C. & W. Co. 2-car DMU picks up some passengers on a service from Edinburgh Waverly to Galashiels on 27th January 1962, before closure of the line. *Douglas Hume*

#325 Unidentified BR Type 4 1Co-Co1 D.E. repainted in unflattering all over rail blue with yellow ends, shrouds the rest of its train with leaking steam from its train heating system as it stops at GALASHIELS during December 1968 with an Edinburgh Waverley to London St. Pancras service, shortly before closure of the famous Waverley route between Edinburgh and Carlisle. *G.N. Turnbull*

#326 BR Type 4 1Co-Co1 D.E. #D24 crosses over with a northbound DMU service at DUNRAGIT as it heads the afternoon Glasgow St. Enoch to Stranraer on the 15th July 1961. This was the first time a "peak" class locomotive was on this route of the former GSWR system. Note the camping coaches in the adjacent siding. This location was near to the golden sandy beaches of Luce Bay on the coast of Galloway, and the camping coaches were popular with holidaymakers in the summer.
Douglas Hume

#327 BR Swindon 6-car DMU splutters away from STRANRAER HARBOUR station with a service for Glasgow St. Enoch in July 1964. Noticeable in this view of the bygone railway age are the recently completed tsss Caledonian Princess, 3630g.r.t., built by the former Wm. Denny & Bros. Ltd. shipyard at Dumbarton. Also of interest are many new motor cars being delivered to Ireland, along with carflat, conflat, cattle and mineral wagons in the adjoining sidings.
WAC Smith/TTT

Section 6
Junctions

At the time of the formation of B.R., the Scottish Region contained several hundred railway junctions. These locations were thus defined because they were the points of convergence of many lines, and were invariably controlled by adjacent and manually operated signal boxes. Their conception and development were inextricably linked to that of the initial types of mechanical signalling and control systems. Their irrefutable necessity became the embodiment of the safe signalling operating rationale of railway systems, not only in Britain but throughout the world.

As traditional manually operated signals and points were gradually replaced by colour light signals and interlocked electro pneumatic pointwork, so too did the wholesale rationalisation of intricate junction trackwork proceed, along with the eradication of hundreds of traditional signal boxes whose functions thereafter were replaced by a much smaller number of complicated signalling control centres.

Several of the railway junctions which were once synonymous with the B.R. map of routes in Scotland have been illustrated in this section. An attempt has been made to depict graphically the complicated trackwork of yore, alongside the progressive rationalisation which took place thereafter. Subsequent contraction of traffic flows and the advent of long-distance electronic signal control systems ultimately led to extensive track simplification at all of the railway junctions which remained in use.

LIST OF LOCATIONS ILLUSTRATED

#328 BR Type 2 Bo-Bo D.E. #D5117 brings the three coach portion from Thurso into GEORGEMAS JUNCTION on 8th July 1969. The locomotive will move this rake through the station, then propel the three coaches onto the rear of the train from Wick, whence all will be coupled up, (except the Loco from Thurso) to form the regular service train consist for Inverness. *Jack Kernahan*

#329 NBL Type 2 Bo-Bo D.E. #D6155 leaves CAIRNIE JUNCTION with an Elgin to Aberdeen service in June 1965. Note the rakes of mainly Blue Spot insul fish vans stored in the sidings to the left. The rear coach of a service to Elgin via Keith and the Glen line can be seen in the station platform beyond, and to the right is a 2 coach Cravens DMU stabled in a siding. *Roy M.B. Crombie/SRPS*

#330 MAUD JUNCTION on 21st September 1963. On the left is a Cravens 2-car DMU on a St. Combs to Aberdeen service, and on the right is NBL Type 2 Bo-Bo D.E. #D6139 on a service from Peterhead to Maud Junction. Note how tidy is the platform surface with no evidence of dropped litter, or that filthy scourge of the twenty first century, impregnated chewing gum. *Douglas Hume*

#331 NBL type 2 Bo-Bo D.E.s #D6113 and D6129 pass GUTHRIE JUNCTION with a Glasgow Buchanan Street to Aberdeen express on 18th April 1962, before these engines were replaced by the Gresley ex-LNER A4 pacifics. The line in the foreground goes to Arbroath via St.Vigeans. *W.S. Sellar*

#332 DYCE on 31st January 1979, when the line to Fraserburgh seen curving off to the right was still open for freight only. Thundering through the then closed station is a four car DMU hybrid combination from Inverness to Aberdeen comprised of a BR Swindon 3-car DMU with a Gloucester R.C. & W. Co diesel railcar trailing. *Geo. C. O'Hara*

#333BR Type 2 Bo-Bo D.E. #25244 trundles a rake of almost new four wheel air braked wagons conveying agricultural lime from Coxhoe, on the North Eastern Region onto the truncated former Strathmore line, at KINNABER JUNCTION, bound for Brechin on 11th November 1980. *Geo. C. O'Hara*

STANLEY JUNCTION

PREVIOUS PAGE:
#334 BALLINLUIG JUNCTION on 23rd April 1965 with BR Type 2 Bo-Bo D.E. #D5126 and a one coach over-powered mock railbus service from Aberfeldy in the bay platform to the left, and a Metro-Cammell 2-car DMU on the up main line platform with a service from Blair Atholl to Perth. Note the goods yard and goods shed beyond the station footbridge. *Douglas Hume*

#335 The second man of BRCW Type 2 Bo-Bo D.E. #D5335 at the head of a northbound goods collects the tablet from the signalman at STANLEY JUNCTION for the next northern section of the former HR main line during February 1962. *Norris Forrest/TTT*

#336 The signalman at CONNEL FERRY JUNCTION looks extremely despondent as he walks out from his signal box to exchange the token with the crew of an unidentified BRCW Type 2 Bo-Bo D.E. taking the line to Ballachulish on the last day of service on the Argyllshire branch line, 26th March 1966. *Alan Carlaw*

#337 METHVEN JUNCTION is visited by members of a Glasgow University Railtour on a hot and pleasant day in May 1961, when the traction provided was a D. Wickham 4-wheel diesel railbus #SC79968, and the short Perthshire branch was still open for goods and mineral traffic. *Roy M.B. Crombie/SRPS*

#338 Metro-Cammell 2-car DMU splutters onto the main line at KINROSS JUNCTION with a service from Stirling to Perth via the Devon Valley line on 1st February 1964. Note the loading dock in the adjacent siding, presumably used for the transit of livestock. *Douglas Hume*

#339 ALLOA EAST JUNCTION and the intricate diamond crossing from the Devon Valley line trailing in from the right is traversed by BRCW Type 2 Bo-Bo D.E. #D5317 in charge of an afternoon stopping service from Stirling to Edinburgh Waverley on 6th October 1962. Note the unidentified ex NBR 0-6-0 J36 loco with empty mineral wagon in the siding, and unidentified BR 0-6-0 350 h.p. D.E. shunter in the left foreground.
WAC Smith/TTT

#340 ALLOA JUNCTION on 27th January 1968 is passed by Park Royal 4-wheel diesel railbus #SC79977 as it makes its way from Larbert to Alloa via Throsk, and the Alloa swing bridge. *Jack Kernahan*

#341 Metro-Cammell 2-car DMU at COWDENBEATH NORTH JUNCTION with a service from Perth to Edinburgh Waverley on 15th November 1969. Note the trailing points still to be released after the clearance by the junction signal.

Douglas Hume

#342 BR Derby 3-car DMU on a service for Dundee Tay Bridge approaches LEUCHARS JUNCTION where the bay platform usually despatches the service to St. Andrews in July 1966.

Roy M.B. Crombie/SRPS

#343 BR 0-6-0 350 h.p. D.E. shunter #D3409 at CARRON JUNCTION with a trip freight working from Denny to Grangemouth on 31st August 1964.

Robin Nelson

#344 Clayton Type 1 Bo-Bo D.E. #D8563 passes BONNINGTON SOUTH JUNCTION with a trip freight working from Granton to Millerhill yard on 18th March 1966. *Robin Nelson*

J#345 EE Type 4 1Co-Co1 D.E. #D241 near MONKTONHALL JUNCTION with the 'up' Heart of Midlothian service from Edinburgh to London on 3rd April 1961. *WAC Smith/TTT*

#346 Metro-Cammell 2-car DMU passes FISHERROW JUNCTION on the short branch from Musselburgh with a service for Edinburgh Waverley on 3rd April 1961. *WAC Smith/TTT*

#347 Glouceste R.C. & W. Co. 4- DMU with a Glasgo Central to Coalbu service approach BLACKWOO JUNCTION on 14t April 1962. The branc to the left was part a once extensi network of lines whi used to service son of the collieries of t Lanarkshire coalfie and rejoined the li to Coalburn about fi miles north at Merr ton Junction. The la working coal mine this part of Lanarkshi was Auchlochan collie near Coalburn whi closed in 1968.

WAC Smith/T

#348 Cravens 2-car DMU leaves STONEHOUSE JUNCTION with a service from Glasgow Central to Strathaven in October 1964. The signal box in the distance controlled the pointwork on the line to Coalburn which branched off to the left.

Roy M.B. Crombie/SRPS

#349 NBL Type Bo-Bo D.E. #D61 approaches the tri track convergence FULLWOOD JUN TION with a serv from Coatbri Central to Holyto on the 15th Octo 1962.

WAC Smith/T

#350 Cravens 2-car DMU passes PARTICK EAST JUNCTION with a service from Kilbowie to Rutherglen on 18th September 1964. Note the rake of seemingly well maintained vacuum fitted cattle wagons about to be tripped to nearby Merklands Lairage on the adjacent Clydeside Tramway situated about half a mile beyond the tall structure of Meadowside Granary which was built by the former Clyde Navigation Trust in 1936. *Roy Hamilton*

#351 BR Swindon 6-car DMU passes GERMISTON JUNCTION and an unidentified ex-LMS 4-6-0 class 5 locomotive stopped at signal check as it heads east with a diverted service from Glasgow Buchanan Street in January 1961. *WAC Smith/TTT*

#352 GORBAL JUNCTION on 23r August 1964 with a unidentified Clayto Type 1 Co-Co D. hauling a rake of emp coaching stock fro Glasgow St. Enoc while a pair of B Standard Class 4 2-6 tanks haul a simil working. *Robin Nels*

#353 Clayton Type Co-Co D.E. #D85 passes GORBA JUNCTION with service from Glasgo St. Enoch to Ea Kilbride on 27 August 1964.

Robin Nels

#354 EE Type 1 Bo- D.E. #20099 propels rake of empty vacu fitted 16 ton mine wagons into Yoker ya at CLYDEBAN DOCK JUNCTIC where they will tripped to Dalmuir be loaded with scr steel from the W. Arnott Young Ltd., sh breaking yard on t 30th March 1979.

Geo. C. O'H

#355 The much contracted and rationalised SCOTSTOUN WEST JUNCTION on 19th January 1978 after a recent snow flurry, as BR 0-6-0 350 h.p. D.E. shunter #08718 heads for Yoker yard with six empty fuel oil tanks from Partick Central. Noticeable in this view of Glasgow are many new vehicles from the former Albion Motors Ltd. works occupying the solum of what once was Scotstoun West yard. The platform edge can still be seen of the former passenger station of the same name on the truncated branch to Old Kilpatrick fuel depot. *Geo. C. O'Hara*

#356 BRCW Type 2 Bo-Bo D.E. #27105 approaches KNIGHTSWOOD NORTH JUNCTION with the daily Cadder Yard to Fort William fitted mixed goods on 10th April 1980. The interesting consist of steam era vacuum fitted 4-wheel wagons comprise BR abbreviations of Minfit, Covhop and Plate VB. Note the Forth and Clyde canal to the right of this view. *Geo. C. O'Hara*

#357 EE Type 1 Bo-Bo D.E. #D8127 passes COWLAIRS NORTH JUNCTION with an Edinburgh Waverley to Balloch Pier excursion on 1st July 1963. Note the tall reinforced concrete coaling tower of Eastfield Loco shed beyond.
Douglas Hume

#358 EE Type 3 Co-Co D.E. #37065 descends from the short branch to Dalmuir Riverside at the new CLYDEBANK JUNCTION with the daily trip working from the nearby Chivas Brothers Ltd. bottling plant to the company's distillery at Keith via Mossend yard on 14th June 1990. *Geo. C. O'Hara*

#359 BR Swindon 3-car DMU passes IBROX JUNCTION where the Govan branch is seen veering off to the right, with a service from Ayr to Glasgow St. Enoch in June 1965.
Roy M.B. Crombie/SRPS

#360 EE Type 3 Co-Co D.E. #37196 takes a short rake of four-wheel molasses air braked tank wagons down the branch to James Watt Dock United Molasses Co. Ltd. siding at INCHGREEN JUNCTION on 2nd November 1987. The trackbed in the foreground formerly served a siding used by the Scott-Lithgow Ltd. shipbuilding and engineering conglomerate for the delivery each week of several hundred tons of steel plates and sections. *Geo. C. O'Hara*

#361 BR Swindon 3-car DMU passes SHIELDHALL JUNCTION with a service from Stranraer to Glasgow Central on 3rd April 1980, while EE Type 3 Co-Co D.E. #37129 waits to join the main line with a short train of air braked Cartic wagons conveying some new Talbot Sunbeam motor cars which had been built at the nearby Linwood car plant. *Geo. C. O'Hara*

#362 BR Type 4 1Co-Co1 D.E. #50 "King's Shropshire Light Infantry" minus its D prefix, but still in possession of its cast name plates, now re-painted in BR corporate all over rail blue with full yellow ends approaches DALRY JUNCTION with a lengthy Leeds to Glasgow Central service made up of BR MK1 coaching stock in rail blue/grey livery on 21st July 1973. *Derek Cross*

#363 Brush Type 4 Co-Co D.E. #1895 bereft of its D prefix, but still in grimy two tone green livery at DALRY JUNCTION with an ICI block train of anhydrous ammonia from the company's Haverton Hill, on Teesside chemical works to their Ardeer explosives plant on 21st July 1973. *Derek Cross*

#364 Gloucester R.C. & W. Co. 2-car DMU passes CROSSHOUSE JUNCTION with a service from Glasgow St. Enoch to Kilmarnock via the Garnock Valley line and Irvine on 29th December 1962. Note the height of both home signals, on both 'up' lines which was necessary to allow drivers "sight of the road" because of the road over bridge near the station.
Douglas Hume

#365 BR 0-6-0 350 h.p. D.E. shunter #08344 passes HOLM JUNCTION with a lengthy trip freight of mainly four-wheel vacuum fitted gunpowder vans, barrier wagons and a pair of 'top and tail' brake vans from Ardrossan yard to Bogside on 6th April 1981.
Geo. C. O'Hara

#366 Unidentified EE Type 3 Co-Co D.E. takes the Kilmarnock line at BARASSIE JUNCTION with an Ayr Falkland yard to Carlisle Speedlink service in June 1988, as an unidentified sister loco idles in the adjacent loop with the Grangemouth to BP Riccarton (Kilmarnock) oil tanks.
Geo. C. O'Hara

#367 EE Type 1 Bo-Bo D.E.s #D8092 and #D8318 coupled unusually with both bonnets facing outwards, come off the branch system to Killoch and Littlemill Collieries at ANNBANK JUNCTION with a trainload of graded coal in 16 ton unfitted mineral wagons on 11th August 1971.
Derek Cross

#368 An unidentified EE Type 1 Bo-Bo D.E. approaches the crossover at ANNBANK JUNCTION with a trainload of coal from Barony Colliery in a rake of very new looking HBA air-braked wagons bound for Ayr harbour on 26th February 1982.
Geo. C. O'Hara

#369 Unusual super power at NEWTON JUNCTION, Ayr as EE Type 4 Co-Co D.E.s #425 and #449 prepare to take the line to Mauchline with a severely diverted Glasgow Central to London Euston express on 14th November 1971.
Derek Cross

#370 Brush Type 4 Co-Co D.E. #1881 (shorn of its D prefix, but still in two tone green livery) takes the Kilmarnock line at MAUCHLINE JUNCTION with a Haverton Hill on Tees to Ardeer ICI block train of anhydrous ammonia vacuum fitted tank wagons on 24th July 1971.
Derek Cross

#371 Gloucester R.C. & W. Co. 2-car DMU leaves INCHES station, junction of the short Carmacoup branch to the National Coal Board Kennox Colliery, the line to which is seen climbing gradually to the left, on 3rd October 1964 with a service from Muirkirk to Lanark shortly before closure of the line. *WAC Smith/TTT*

#372 EE Type 4 1Co-Co1 D.E. #40058 glides past DALRYMPLE JUNCTION with a trainload of new cars and vans for Stranraer (and Northern Ireland) on 9th April 1982. The line to the right runs to Waterside open cast rail loading facility and is about ten miles long. *Geo. C. O'Hara*

#373 BRCW Type 2 Bo-Bo D.E. #D5338 passes KELSO JUNCTION, near St. Boswells on the former Waverley Route with a Carlisle to Edinburgh service on 7th July 1963.
Douglas Hume

#374 BR Type 2 Bo-Bo D.E. #25230 awaits the passing of an unidentified Brush Type 4 Co-Co D.E. on a Glasgow Central to Carlisle stopping service at MAXWELLTON JUNCTION with a trip freight from the ICI works at Cargenbridge to ICI Powfoot on 12th July 1984.
Geo. C. O'Hara

#375 Gloucester R.C. & W. Co. 2-car DMU approaches KILNKNOWE JUNCTION with an Edinburgh Waverley to Galashiels via Peebles service on 27th January 1962, which was the last day of the passenger service. *Douglas Hume*

#376 Metro-Cammell 8-car DMU at RICCARTON JUNCTION with a special Ramblers Railtour working over the former Border Counties railway from Newcastle to Scotland via Kielder on 7th September 1959. Note the extensive rake of antiquated cattle wagons in the bay siding.

Douglas Hume

#377 BR Swindon 6-car DMU from Stranraer to Glasgow St. Enoch starts the long climb to Barrhill at CHALLOCH JUNCTION in June 1964, when the former Port Road to Dumfries, seen veering off to the right, was still open. *WAC Smith/TTT*

#378 BRCW Type 2 Bo-Bo D.E. #D5304 leaves RIDDINGS JUNCTION, (actually in England) but junction for the former Langholm branch, with a Carlisle to Edinburgh Waverley service on 25th April 1964. The viaduct carrying the line to Langholm can be seen crossing near the convergence of rivers Esk and Liddle as they become the River Esk thence flow into the Solway Firth. *Roy Hamilton*

Section 7
Locomotive Hauled Goods Trains

This transition in locomotive traction from steam to diesel was implemented in parallel with that of passenger train modernisation. All classes of Type 4 1Co-Co1 D.E's did not haul freight workings until there were sufficient numbers of Brush Type 4 Co-Co D.E's. operating reliably throughout the network. The entire inventory of Type 2 Bo-Bo D.E's hauled both types of trains. The remarkable reliability of the ubiquitous E.E. Type 1 Bo-Bo- D.E's saw these engines pressed into occasional passenger train haulage, especially for specials and railtours in the summer when no train heating facilities were needed.

Towards the end of the era that was British Railways, double heading of goods trains became very common on the former Scottish Region. Several factors initiated this type of working practice, notably the year on year reduction in tonnages of freight carried, released locomotives which had become surplus. Additionally the need for more assured reliability in timekeeping on shared track became critical as concurrent passenger train working timetables were accelerated in a concerted effort by B.R. management to redress the falling public profile of rail travel.

Despite these attempts at improved freight train service timings, and the introduction of the popular, efficient and well-supported Speedlink Network, along with a plethora of air-braked high speed custom built freight wagons, country wide freight haulage on the B.R. Scottish Region was allowed to decay to the point where only a handful of bulk or large volume freight flows remained with British Railways at the time of "piratisation".

Like the previous section on diesel powered passenger trains, the following spread of photographs illustrates all of the classes of former B.R. diesel locomotives hauling a variety of former freight services which were once common sights on the once extensive network of B.R. Scottish Region. These pictures are laid out from north to south.

If the N.B.L. Type 2 Bo-Bo D.E.s were the nadir of Scottish designed and built diesel electric locomotives, then the Clayton Type 1 Bo-Bo D.E.s were their English equivalent. Definitely the most distinctive design of diesel ever to have graced the B.R. network, their abysmal performance consigned them to a troublesome and truncated operational career, usually always double headed in anticipation of their predicated unreliability and inevitable breakdown.

LIST OF LOCATIONS ILLUSTRATED

#379 BR Type 2 Bo-Bo D.E. #D5118 growls away from Helmsdale with a nicely mixed freight of steam era vans and wagons from Inverness to Wick and Thurso, and the stations in between on 8th July 1969. Note the rake of empty Blue Spot insul fish vans in the middle of the consist returning to Wick. *Jack Kernahan*

#380 BRCW Type 2 Bo-Bo D.E. #26039 begins the climb from Ardgay to Culrain with the lengthy daily mixed pick-up goods train from Inverness to Wick and Thurso on 13th July 1979. Note the grimy, once white Blue Spot insul fish van in the consist being returned to Wick. *Geo. C. O'Hara*

#381 BR Type 2 Bo-Bo D.E. #D5116 leaves the halt at Attadale with the Inverness to Kyle of Lochalsh mixed goods train containing mainly 12 ton ventilated vanfit wagons on 9th July 1969. *Jack Kernahan*

#382 BRCW Type 2 Bo-Bo D.E. #26039 re-starts the daily Inverness to Wick and Thurso daily pick-up goods train from its stop and shunt at Dingwall on 2nd May 1980. Note the junction signal post for the line to Kyle of Lochalsh to the right. *Geo. C. O'Hara*

#383 BRCW Type 2 Bo-Bo D.E. #26036 passes the Distillers Company Ltd. rail connected grain terminal at Muir of Ord containing about forty 35-ton vacuum fitted bulk grain wagons, alas all now devoid of their once attractive whisky brand hoardings, while hauling a trainload of tank wagons to the B.P. Lairg fuel oil depot on 3rd August 1981. *Geo. C. O'Hara*

#384 Unidentified BRCW Type 2 Bo-Bo D.E. leaves Inverness hauling a contractors special train conveying pipes and refractory bricks for use in the construction of the new British Aluminium Company aluminium smelter at Invergordon during July 1970.
Geo. C. O'Hara

#385 BR Type 2 Bo-Bo D.E. #D5123 brings a northbound mixed goods into Dava station on the former HR main line during June 1965. *Roy M.B. Crombie/SRPS*

#386 The same train as depicted in #385 is seen crossing the impressive viaduct over the infant River Divie near Dunphail in June 1965. *Roy M.B. Crombie/SRPS*

#387 Unidentified BR Type 2 Bo-Bo D.E. stops at Dunphail with a northbound goods on the former HR main line to await the crossing of a southbound train in July 1965. *Norris Forrest/TTT*

#388 EE Type 1 Bo-Bo D.E. #D8032 leaves Craigellachie and trundles south along the valley of the River Spey with the southbound daily pick-up goods working on 29th June 1966. *John M. Boyes – The Armstrong Railway Photographic Trust*

389 EE Type 1 Bo-Bo .E. #D8031 rolls into arron to pick up the oken for the next section f the line, with the daily ick-up goods from raigellachie on 30th June 966.

John M. Boyes – The Armstrong Railway Photographic Trust

#390 Unidentified EE Type 1 Bo-Bo D.E. skirts the A95 road between Cromdale and Advie with a lengthy southbound Speyside goods train consisting mainly of vanfits on 11th July 1961.
John Spencer Gilks

#391 With the exhaust plumes from both locomotives visible from their combined horse power of 2750 h.p. EE Type 1 Bo-Bo D.E. #20.126 pilots unidentified EE Type 3 Co-Co D.E. through Dalwhinnie during September 1983 with a trainload of agricultural lime bound for Inverness loaded in a rake of different types of BR and private owner fitted mineral wagons.
Sandy Murdoch/TTT

#392 EE Type 3 Co-Co D.E. #37260 "Radio Highland" powers past the traditional Scottish whisky distillery at Dalwhinnie with a Millerhill yard to Inverness yard Speedlink service conveying liquified petroleum gas, cement and domestic coal on 27th May 1989. *Tom H. Noble*

#393 In the middle of a pine forest a few miles north of the junction at Alves, EE Type 4 1Co-Co1 D.E. #40103 hauls a lengthy rake of vacuum fitted 35 ton empty bulk grain wagons from Burghead, bound for Doncaster Belmont yard on 28th June 1977. *Geo. C. O'Hara*

#394 BR Type 2 Bo-Bo D.E. #D5127 passes through Blair Atholl with a down Blue Circle cement train consisting of a long rake of functional Presflo wagons adorned with the attractive company logo hoarding in June 1968. *Roy M.B. Crombie/SRPS*

#395 BR Type 2 Bo-Bo D.E. #25044 storms through the site of the former station at Kinaldie with an Elgin to Aberdeen nicely mixed Speedlink air-braked service on 30th April 1980. *Geo. C. O'Hara*

#396 EE Type 3 Co-Co D.E. #37110 near Kinaldie with a Roisele to Aberdeen Speedlink service of three Polybulk grain wagons on 24th May 1988. *Geo. C. O'Hara*

#397 The peak of Bennachie (1733 ft) is prominent against the Aberdeenshire skyline as BRCW Type 2 Bo-Bo D.E. #26044 rattles an exhaust strewn rake of vacuum fitted bulk grain wagons from Burghead to Doncaster east of Kintore on 28th June 1979. *Geo. C. O'Hara*

#398 Unusual locomotive combination of unidentified EE Type 4 1Co-Co1 D.E. and BR Type 2 Bo-Bo D.E. seen west of Dyce with an Elgin to Aberdeen Speedlink air-braked mixed freight service on 28th June 1979. *Geo. C. O'Hara*

#399 NBL Type 2 Bo-Bo D.E. #D6147 pulls away from Maud Junction with a lengthy rake of conflat wagons loaded with insulated containers and Blue Spot insul fish vans from Fraserburgh and Peterhead bound for London Billingsgate market on 9th July 1960. Note the extensive amount of stored vans, insul fish vans and conflats in the adjacent sidings.

Roy Hamilton

#400 EE Type 1 Bo-Bo D.E. #D8029 arrives at Maud Junction with a mixed goods working from Peterhead conveying presumably an unfunctional passenger coach being taken to Inverurie works for examination in July 1965.

Sandy Murdoch/TTT

#401 Unidentified NBL Type 2 Bo-Bo D.E. south of Fraserburgh with a fish train in November 1964. The track of the short unfenced branch line to St. Combs trails off to the right.

WAC Smith/TTT

#402 NBL Type 2 Bo-Bo D.E. #D6148 passes a newly ploughed field near Brucklay with a southbound Buchan Line fitted van train during March 1965. *Sandy Murdoch/TTT*

#403 Clayton Type 1 Bo-Bo D.E. #D8604 near Mintlaw with a fitted van train conveying produce from the Crosse & Blackwell foodstuffs plant at Peterhead in June 1965. *Sandy Murdoch/TTT*

#404 NBL Type 2 Bo-Bo D.E. #D6143 heads an empty van train for Peterhead, including three empty Blue Spot insul fish vans, west of Mintlaw in November 1965. *Sandy Murdoch/TTT*

#405 EE Type 1 Bo-Bo D.E. #D8031 passes the western suburbs of Aberdeen with a goods train from Ballater and the other Deeside Line intermediate goods yards on 14th April 1960. *Sandy Edward/GNSRA*

#406 EE Type 1 Bo-Bo D.E. #D8028 near Ruthrieston with a Deeside Line pick-up goods train from Ballater to Aberdeen on 27th February 1960. *Sandy Edward/GNSRA*

#407 Unidentified EE Type 4 1Co-Co1 powers round the curve at Kinnaber Junction where the line is still connected to the town of Brechin, with a well loaded Aberdeen to London Freightliner service on 5th September 1978.
Geo. C. O'Hara

#408 Displaying its number on the bufferbeam, Clayton Type 1 Bo-Bo D.E. #D8618 brings a rake of empty unfitted 16-ton mineral wagons towards the west end of Dundee in June 1965, presumably to be worked over the Tay Bridge and destined for some colliery in Fife.
Sandy Murdoch/TTT

#409 Clayton Type 1 Bo-Bo D.E. #D8564 and #D8560 pass through Bridge of Earn with a Millerhill yard to Perth yard fitted freight on 23rd May 1964. *Roy Hamilton*

#410 The driver of BR Type 2 Bo-Bo D.E. #25033 salutes the photographer as his slow moving mixed goods train from Thornton Junction to Dundee, containing eight Blue Spot insul fish vans passes Lochmuir Box on 25th June 1975. *Morrison Bryce*

#411 EE Type 4 1Co-Co1 D.E. #40165 brings a rake of laden fitted and unfitted 16-ton mineral wagons with coal from Seafield Colliery into Oakley yard, for de-gasification at the Rexco plant on the branch to Comrie Colliery during January 1977. *Geo. C. O'Hara*

#412 BRCW Type 2 Bo-Bo D.E. #26023 climbs past the rail connected Clatchard Craig Quarry near Newburgh, with a Perth yard to Millerhill yard Speedlink service on 10th July 1986. *Geo. C. O'Hara*

#413 Brush Type 5 Co-Co D.E. #56074 "Kellingley Colliery" climbs out of Inverkeithing towards the Forth Bridge with a rake of MGR wagons laden with coal from Westfield to Millerhill yard on 13th September 1990. *Tom H. Noble*

#414 Unidentified BRCW Type 2 Bo-Bo D.E. passes above the beach at Burntisland thronging with holidaymakers in June 1964, as it conveys a fitted goods train bound for Millerhill yard. The spur to the right foreground led to the extensive railway sidings which served the docks and shipyard in the Fife town. *Sandy Murdoch/TTT*

#415 A pair of unidentified BRCW Type 2 Bo-Bo D.E.s approach Touch East Junction at Dunfermline with a northbound mixed goods working from Millerhill yard to Perth during June 1965. In the distance are the pylons of East End Park, home of Dunfermline Athletic Football Club, also known as the 'Pars'. *WAC Smith/TTT*

#416 Clayton Type 1 Bo-Bo D.E. #D8570 in rail blue livery heads a fitted goods train at Seafield, Leith on 16th April 1968. The signals to the left were sighting signals for the testing of drivers' eyesight. *Hamish Stevenson*

#417 Brush Type 5 Co-Co D.E. #60077 "Canisp" crawls along the speed restricted Powderhall Branch with an empty 'bin liner' working from Kaimes disposal site on 15th April 1993. The train is seen passing the rear of the former Edinburgh Corporation Tramways Shrubhill works. *Max Fowler*

#418 Brush Type 5 Co-Co D.E. #60049 "Scafell" powers the BSC Dalzell plate mill to Lackenby, Teesside train of empty BBA empty steel slab carrying wagons near Blindwells during November 1992. *Max Fowler*

#419 EE Type 4 1Co-Co1 D.E. #40063 departs from the former Freightliner terminal at Portobello with a service to Cardiff, containing many kegs of premium Scottish brewed beer and lager on 16th April 1981. *Morrison Bryce*

#420 EE Type 4 1Co-Co1 D.E. #40195 passes Innerwick, near Dunbar, with an ICI company train conveying anhydrous ammonia from Haverton Hill on Tees to Leith on 18th September 1981. Note the use of redundant insul fish vans being used as barrier wagons behind the locomotive. *Morrison Bryce*

#421 BRCW Type 2 Bo-Bo D.E. #D5331 prepares to leave Crieff yard with a mixed goods working to Perth yard on 4th March 1966. Regular goods and mineral traffic to and from this attractive Perthshire town lasted until September 1967.
Sandy Smeaton

#422 NBL Type 2 Bo-Bo D.E.s #D6120 and D6109 approach Bridge of Allan with a train for the Callander and Oban line consisting mainly of alumina from Burntisland bound for Ballachulish on 2nd March 1963. The leading locomotive grill seems somewhat oil splattered, a noticeable fault of some of these stylish yet unreliable Glasgow built engines.
Derek Cross

#423 BRCW Type 2 Bo-Bo D.E. #27205 passes through Stirling with a very mixed Speedlink service from Thornton Junction to Mossend yard via Alloa on 2nd April 1980. Note the extensive amount of vanfits in the adjacent sidings.
Morrison Bryce

#424 The dirty windows of NBL Type 2 Bo-Bo D.E. #D6122 replicate a pair of eyes as it passes Throsk signal box where the token for the Alloa swing bridge is exchanged. The train is a fitted goods from Alloa yard to Mossend yard on 9th July 1966. The branch in the left foreground served the R.N. supply depot at Bandeath. *Roy Hamilton*

#425 EE Type 3 Co-Co D.E. #37147 looking far from resplendent in weathered and grimy rail blue livery, leaves Grangemouth yard with a southbound train of tanks from the B.P. refinery on 7th March 1980. *Geo. C. O'Hara*

#426 Clayton Type 1 Bo-Bo D.E.s #D8538 in rail blue, and an unidentified sister locomotive breast the summit of the Benhar branch, also called Starryshaw, with a trainload of coking coal from Polkemmet Colliery at Whitburn in the mid 1960's. *WAC Smith/TTT*

#427 EC Type 4 1Co-Co1 D.E. #40098 passes Hillend Reservoir with a lengthy trainload of new cars from Luton to the Bathgate distribution railhead on 19th March 1980, by which time the line had been singled prior to it being lifted a few years later. *Morrison Bryce*

8S53

PREVIOUS PAGE:
#428 Brush Type 5 Co-Co D.E. #60091 "An Teallach" passes Carstairs H.M. Government Correction Centre with a Millerhill yard to Ravenstruther coal loading terminal empty MGR working on 26th June 1992. *Max Fowler*

#429 EE Type 4 Co-Co D.E. #432 (minus its D prefix) and with very little exhaust plume, near Baillieston with a freight from Mossend yard to Carlisle on 14th July 1972, an unusual working for the locomotive. *WAC Smith/TTT*

#430 Triple heading of unidentified EE Type 1 Bo-Bo D.E. and a pair of EE Type 3 Co-Co D.E.s pass through Mossend yard with a rake of BSC loaded bogie iron ore tipplers from Hunterston bound for Ravenscraig on 10th May 1982. *Morrison Bryce*

#431 BRCW Type 2 Bo-Bo D.E. #27024 hauls a trainload of steel pipes from BSC Clydesdale Tube Mill seen in the background bound for the nearby BSC Imperial Tube (finishing) works at Airdrie on 19th April 1982. *Morrison Bryce*

432 BRCW Type 2 o-Bo D.E. #D5366 eads a lengthy Mallaig ound mixed goods ain conveying a variety f different types of sul fish vans, west of lenfinnan in June 1962. *Roy M.B. Crombie/SRPS*

433 EE Type 3 Co-Co E. #37108 between rianlarich and Tyndrum pper with the Alcan ompany train conying alumina from yth to Fort William on th August 1984. These agons used to be used r the transport of ain. *Tom H. Noble*

#434 EE Type 3 Co-Co D.E. #37146 growls along the north side of Strathfillan towards Tyndrum Upper with the daily timber train from Crianlarich to Corpach on 2nd May 1979. The snow rutted Munros of Ben More (3852 ft) left, and Stob Binnein (3821 ft) centre, are prominent in the left distance.
Geo. C. O'Hara

#435 BRCW Type 2 Bo-Bo D.E. #5390 threads the Monessie Gorge near Spean Bridge with the daily Crianlarich to Corpach timber train on 26th July 1973. *Morrison Bryce*

#436 EE Type 3 Co-Co D.E. #37028 skirts the plantings of a future timber harvest near Tyndrum Upper with a Crianlarich to Corpach timber train on 27th April 1979. These vacuum fitted Timber P wagons shown in all three of these photographs were built on the chassis of redundant plate wagons at the former B.R. wagon works at Barrassie, Troon.
Geo. C. O'Hara

PREVIOUS PAGE:
#437 BRCW Type 2 Bo-Bo D.E. #D5363 waits at Garelochhead with a Yoker Yard to Fort William mixed goods train to allow the passing of a southbound passenger train on the searing hot and hazy day of 8th June 1965. *Robin Nelson*

#438 BR Type 2 Bo-Bo D.E. #25044 leaves the loops at Craigendoran and joins the West Highland Line with a fitted Speedlink service for Fort William and Corpach pulp mill on 8th May 1980. *Tom H. Noble*

#439 BRCW Type 2 Bo-Bo D.E. #27009 crosses over the River Leven viaduct at Dumbarton with a Cadder yard to Fort William vacuum fitted goods train conveying six covhop alumina wagons in the consist during December 1979. *Geo. C. O'Hara*

#440 BRCW Type 2 Bo-Bo D.E. #D5356 approaches Kentallen with a Ballachulish to Connel Ferry mixed goods working in May 1963. Note the batch of empty Presflo alumina wagons returning to Burntisland. *Ken Nuttall*

#441 BRCW Type 2 Bo-Bo D.E. #D5356 in charge of the same Ballachulish to Connel Ferry mixed goods train seen above waits at Appin, for a northbound passenger train to clear the section during May 1963. *Ken Nuttall*

#442 BRCW Type 2 Bo-Bo D.E. #D5347 near Tyndrum Lower with an Oban to Glasgow mixed goods on 26th June 1964. Note the six empty Presflo alumina wagons returning from Ballachulish to Burntisland. *J.A.C. Kirke/TTT*

#443 Mist shrouded Ben Cruachan (3695ft) looms over BRCW Type 2 Bo-Bo D.E. #27009 as it heads a small fitted Cadder yard to Oban mixed goods train near Taynuilt on 2nd May 1979. *Geo. C. O'Hara*

#444 Unidentified BRCW Type 2 Bo-Bo D.E. skirts the western side of Loch Lubnaig with a very mixed Oban to Glasgow goods working on a hot and hazy 3rd July 1963. *Robin Nelson*

#445 EE Type 4 1Co-Co1 D.E. #40158 growls through Bowling station with an eastbound oil tank train from the former ESSO fuel oil storage terminal in the same village on 26th March 1980. *Geo. C. O'Hara*

#446 EE Type 1 Bo-Bo D.E. #D8090 passes Lochburn signal box with an 'up' goods train on 10th September 1963. Included within the consist are six wagons of graded coal from Garscube Colliery which was the last pit to be worked in the city of Glasgow, and was located about one mile west of the tenements in the distance. The siding beyond the signal box served the works of the Saracen Foundry where rail traffic ceased in 1964. *WAC Smith/TTT*

#447 A pair of unidentified Clayton Type 1 Bo-Bo D.E.s head a lengthy rake of vacuum fitted iron ore hoppers from Ravenscraig steel works returning to General Terminus Quay in May 1964, and are seen near Bellshill. *WAC Smith/TTT*

#448 BRCW Type 2 Bo-Bo D.E. #27034 passes the steel foundry of R.B. Tennent Ltd. at Whifflet with a mixed freight for Mossend yard on 28th March 1975.
Hamish Stevenson

#449 BRCW Type 2 Bo-Bo D.E. #27111 passes under the trackbed of the former CR Line from Partick West to Possil with a train of mainly VEA vans from Glen Douglas to Mossend yard on 27th March 1980. *Geo. C. O'Hara*

#450 EE Type 3 Co-Co D.E.s #37144 and #37108 crawl up the short branch from Rothesay Dock to Yoker yard with a trainload of imported coking coal for BSC Ravenscraig Steelworks on 11th April 1980. Note the unidentified BR 0-6-0 350 h.p. D.E. shunter banking.
Geo. C. O'Hara

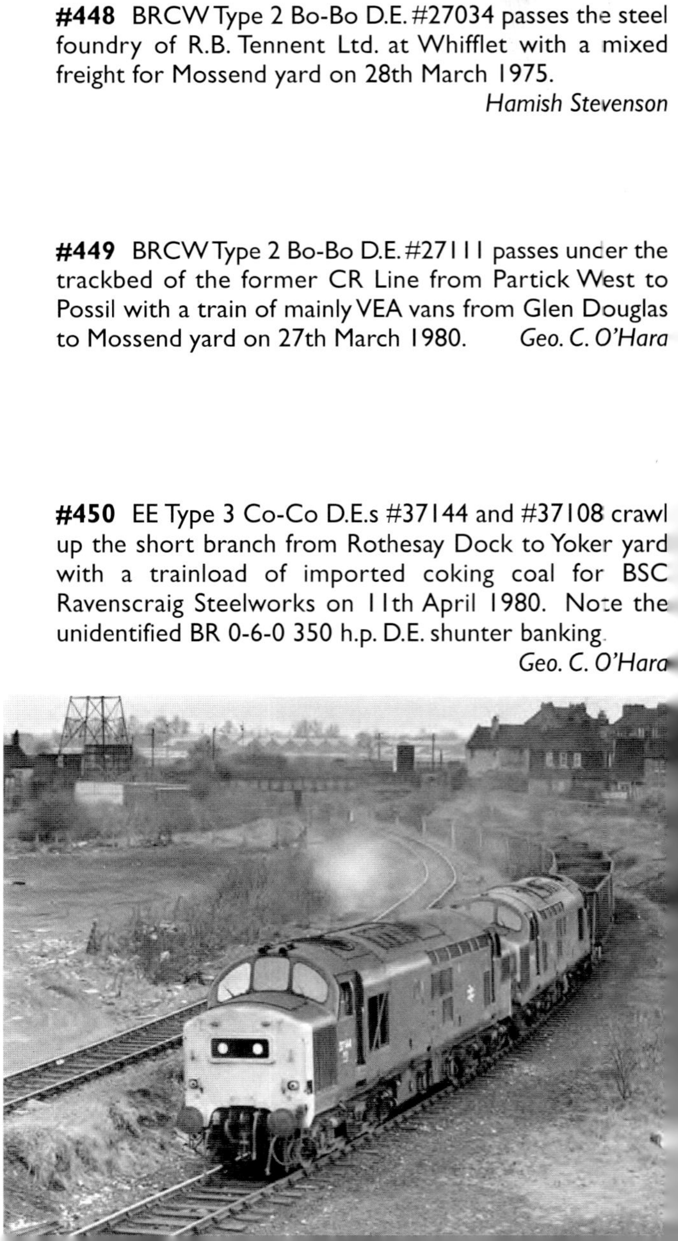

#451 Unidentified Clayton Type 1 Bo-Bo D.E. propels a partly fitted goods train down the short branch towards Kinning Park goods station during a searing June evening in 1964. *Alan Carlaw*

#452 Clayton Type 1 Bo-Bo D.E. #D8553 passes through the single platform station of Hairmyres on the East Kilbride branch with a rake of empty vans from the 'Radio Times' distribution railhead seen on the left of this view on 23rd May 1964. *WAC Smith/TTT*

#453 EE Type 3 Co-Co D.E.s #37081 and #37147 crawl up the short branch from General Terminus Quay with a trainload of imported coking coal for BSC Ravenscraig Steelworks on 28th November 1979. This working took place due to the fact that the new BSC coal and iron ore terminal at Hunterston was not yet operational. *Geo. C. O'Hara*

#454 EE Type 1 Bo-Bo D.E.s #20127 and #20226 lead a container train for the German Hapag Lloyd Shipping line from Coatbridge to the Clyde Port Authority terminal at Greenock on 1st November 1986. Note the cranes of two of the moribund former Greenock Shipyards which were once owned by Scott-Lithgow Ltd.
Geo. C. O'Hara

#455 Observing the speed restriction on the overgrown rump of part of the former branch to Greenock Princes Quay, EE Type 3 Co-Co D.E. #37008 growls past the site of the former Lyndeoch Junction with a rake of empty container flats from the Clyde Port Authority Greenock terminal to Coatbridge on 16th May 1987. *Geo. C. O'Hara*

#456 EE Type 3 Co-Co D.E. #37043 clatters through Port Glasgow with a rake of empty container flats from Greenock CPA Terminal to Coatbridge on 17th May 1986. Noticeable in the background is the giant self propelled semi-submersible drilling rig 'OCEAN ALLIANCE' 15517 g.r.t., on the berth of the former Scott Lithgow Glen shipyard, which was later razed and is now a housing estate. At the time of her construction this vessel was the largest such craft in the world.
Geo. C. O'Hara

#457 EE Type 3 Co-Co D.E. #37144 creates a flurry of exhaust plumes as it leaves R.N.A.D. Giffen with a short Speedlink service to Mossend yard on 7th October 1983.
Geo. C. O'Hara

#458 EE Type 4 1Co-Co1 D.E. #40141 propels its rake of eight SPA air-braked wagons conveying steel ingots from BSC Ravenscraig into the headshunt for BSC Glengarnock Steelworks on 16th April 1981. The empty fuel oil and plate wagons in the adjacent sidings illustrate some of the traditional, extensive types of freight traffic once conveyed by the Scottish Region of British Railways. *Geo. C. O'Hara*

#459 EE Type 3 Co-Co D.E.s #37675 and 37669 take an empty rake of almost brand new china clay slurry tanks (nicknamed silver bullet wagons because of their shiny cladding when introduced in the 1980s) from the Caledonian Paper Co. siding at Shewalton Moss, near Irvine onto the Troon-Kilmarnock line on 21st August 1989. *Tom H. Noble*

PREVIOUS PAGE:
#460 EE Type 1 Bo-Bo D.E.s #20171 and 20127 leave the rail loading bunker at Hunterston on the Largs branch with a trainload of imported coal in a lengthy rake of HAA wagons for BSC Ravenscraig on the 27th April 1987. *Tom H. Noble*

#461 Brush Type 5 Co-Co D.E. #60031 "Ben Lui" near West Kilbride with a trainload of iron-ore from Hunterston to BSC Ravenscraig on 8th April 1992. *Max Fowler*

#462 EE Type 3 Co-Co D.E. #37249 on the Riccarton Branch with a trainload of BP tank wagons from Grangemouth oil refinery for the Hurst Fuels depot at Kilmarnock on 3rd April 1985. *Geo. C. O'Hara*

#463 BR Type 2 Bo-Bo D.E. #25228 clatters a lengthy and nicely mixed Speedlink air-braked service from Ayr Falkland yard to Carlisle through Annbank Junction on 2nd July 1982. *Geo. C. O'Hara*

#464 With the former mining village of Mossblown prominent behind, BRCW Type 2 Bo-Bo D.E. #26039 starts the climb up Tarbolton bank with the weekly nuclear flask train from SSEB Fairlie to UKAE Sellafield storage and re-processing plant on the Cumbrian Coast, on 7th September 1984. *Geo.C. O'Hara*

PREVIOUS PAGE:
#465 Unusual double heading combination of BRCW Type 2 Bo-Bo D.E. #27042 and BR Type 2 Bo-Bo D.E. #25072 cross Enterkine viaduct over the River Ayr with a trainload of HBA hoppers conveying coal from Killoch Colliery to Ayr harbour on 23rd February 1979. *Geo. C. O'Hara*

#466 Late afternoon light conspires to dramatise the effect of BR Type 2 Bo-Bo D.E. #25244 piloting EE Type 1 Bo-Bo D.E. #20089 on the climb up the Ayrshire plateau to Killoch Colliery with a rake of MCV coal empties from Ayr Falkland yard on 23rd February 1982. *Geo. C. O'Hara*

#467 The former goods yard at Muirkirk has seen most of the track recovered and the station and signalbox beyond, about to be demolished as BRCW Type 2 Bo-Bo D.E. #D5365 prepares to haul a trainload of coal from the nearby Kaimes Colliery to Ayr harbour during June 1968. *Derek Cross*

#468 BRCW Type 2 Bo-Bo D.E. #D5364 trundles a trainload of graded coal from either Kaimes Colliery or Cairnhill mine bound for Ayr Falkland yard over the three arch Cronberry viaduct over the Lugar Water during June 1968. *Derek Cross*

#469 BRCW Type 2 Bo-Bo D.E. #26024 (now preserved) north of Prestwick station with a Speedlink service from Ayr Falkland yard on 14th June 1988. Three separate rail connected customers were served by this working, at Irvine, Bogside and Dalry. *Geo. C. O'Hara*

#470 BRCW Type 2 Bo-Bo D.E. #D5352 passes under some of the contraptions of the former NCB Bargany coal mine in the Girvan valley, as it restarts a Stranraer to Glasgow fitted goods train from a signal check on 31st January 1966. *Derek Cross*

#471 With the Firth of Clyde and the island of Arran beyond, EE Type 3 Co-Co D.E. #37193 makes an effortless climb out of Girvan seen below to the left, with a Speedlink service for Stockton Haulage Ltd. conveying a few hundred tonnes of steel sections from Teesside to Stranraer on 3rd January 1985. *Geo. C. O'Hara*

#472 EE Type 1 Bo-Bo D.E. #D8116 trundles towards Polquhap Summit on the GSWR Nith Valley line with a northbound mixed goods train from Carlisle Kingmoor yard on 17th August 1965. *Derek Cross*

#473 BRCW Type 2 Bo-Bo D.E. #26029 powers through New Cumnock with an Ayr Falkland yard to Carlisle Speedlink service conveying several PWA pallet vans used for the transport of fertiliser traffic on 20th June 1986. *Geo. C. O'Hara*

NEXT PAGE:

#474 Unidentified Brush Type 4 Co-Co D.E. slams through Symington with a trainload of slabs loaded onto SSA wagons from BSC Ravenscraig to Bescot yard in the summer of 1969. *Morrison Bryce*

#475 EE Type 4 1Co-Co1 D.E. #40090 labours up Beattock bank near Greskine assisted by a pair of EE Type 1 Bo-Bo D.E.s #20011 and #20114 in charge of a British Oxygen Company Ltd. train conveying liquid oxygen to the former private siding at Polmadie during June 1974. *Morrison Bryce*

#476 BRCW Type 2 Bo-Bo D.E. #D5306 near Riccarton Junction on the former Waverley Route with a Carlisle Kingmoor yard to Millerhill yard fitted freight consisting entirely of 4-wheel vans and wagons on 18th August 1965. *Douglas Hume*

4Z24

Section 8

Mixed Trains

Several of the routes inherited by the Scottish Region of British Railways ran mixed train formations just as former railway companies had done since their inception almost a hundred years previously. Within the fiscal remit of common carrier imposed upon the establishment of B.R, the Scottish Region continued to provide this mixed train service on several mainly branch lines throughout the country. This practice was carried on well beyond the transition to complete dieselisation of the network, and almost up until the time when the entity that was B.R. disappeared.

Initially goods wagons and vans were coupled to the rear of the last passenger coach in the train formation, and a guard's van was attached to the rear of this consist. However, as the inclusion of unfitted rolling stock was gradually phased out, the traffic which was still conveyed in mixed train formations was thence transported in vacuum fitted rolling stock only. These vehicles comprised the inclusion of mainly insul-fish and general merchandise vans, cattle and other livestock wagons, tank wagons and the ubiquitous 16-ton fitted coal wagon in the train formation. As these wagons were now all vacuum operated, their inclusion negated the need for a brake van. Through piping of the vacuum operated brake system also meant that these vehicles could now be coupled next to the locomotive, or at the rear of the train, or even diesel multiple unit, so long as the mandatory tail light was in place on the last wagon, or coach of the train. Only eight Scottish routes which retained mixed

LIST OF LOCATIONS ILLUSTRATED

#477 A local fish merchant supervises the loading of a Blue Spot Insul Fish van in the mixed train consist headed by BRCW Type 2 Bo-Bo D.E. #D5329 at Wick during June 1966, when this practice was a regular type of traffic from the Caithness fishing port. *Roy M.B. Crombie/SRPS*

#478 BR Type 2 Bo-BO D.E. #D5114 shunts a Lowfit loaded with a tractor and a pair of Blue Spot Insul Fish Vans onto the rear of a mixed train consist at Georgemas Junction on 21st June 1960. The Thurso pilot locomotive, an unidentified BRCW Type 2 Bo-Bo D.E. can be seen in the distance beyond the signal box and snow shelter. *Ken Nuttall*

#479 BRCW Type 2 Bo-Bo D.E. #26022 splutters away from Tain with the evening mixed train service from Wick and Thurso to Inverness on 10th June 1980. Note the blackbird perched on a telegraph wire unfazed by the noise and inhalation of engine exhaust fumes. *Geo. C. O'Hara*

#480 A brace of BRCW Type 2 Bo-Bo D.E.s #26039 and #26045 depart from the isolated station at Fearn with the evening Wick and Thurso to Inverness mixed train conveying a single Blue Spot insul fish van on 9th June 1980.

Geo. C. O'Hara

#481 Brush Type 4 Co-Co D.E. #47102 has just shunted a bogie container wagon onto the evening mixed train to Wick and Thurso consist at Inverness on 12th June 1984, not long before this type of traffic was lost to the Far North Line.

Tom H. Noble

#482 BR Type 2 Bo-Bo D.E. #D5120 and BRCW Type 2 Bo-Bo D.E. #D5330 double head a mixed train from Inverness conveying a pair of Blue Spot insul fish vans in the stylish ice blue livery, into Kyle of Lochalsh during June 1968.
Hamish Stevenson Collection/TTT

#483 Unidentified BRCW Type 2 Bo-Bo D.E. shunts the morning mixed train consist from Inverness at Kyle of Lochalsh on 10th July 1978, when the freight vehicle conveyed in the working was a 16-ton vacuum fitted coal wagon.
Geo. C. O'Hara

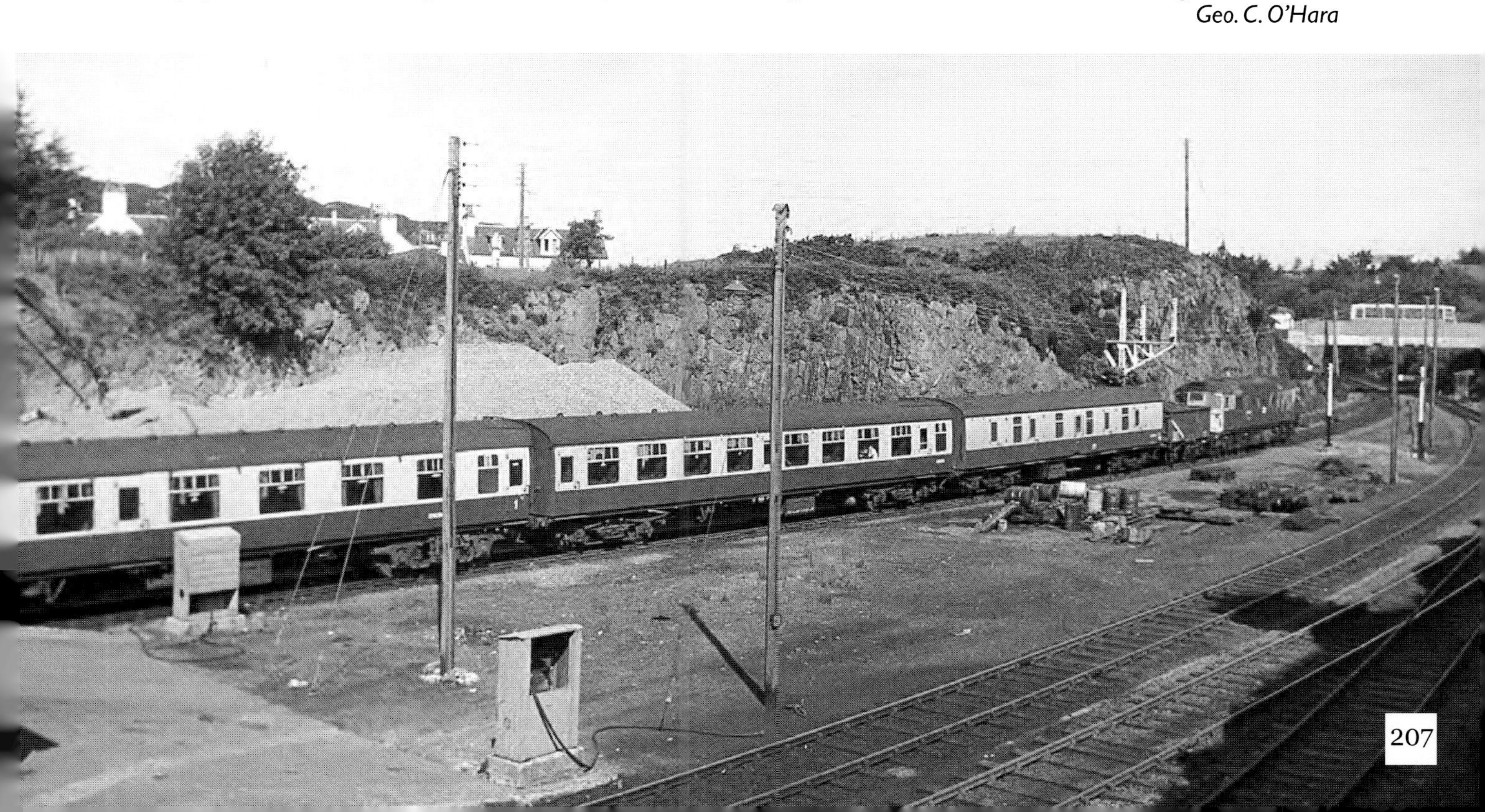

PREVIOUS PAGE: Three views taken at different locations on the beautiful Kyle line by the same photographer of the then regular Kyle of Lochalsh to Inverness mixed train working which contained a pair of Blue Spot insul fish vans.

#484 Unidentified BRCW Type 2 Bo-Bo D.E. heads an eastbound mixed train from Kyle of Lochalsh to Inverness near Duncraig in June 1967. *Roy M.B. Crombie/SRPS*

#485 Unidentified BRCW Type 2 Bo-Bo D.E. heads a Kyle of Lochalsh to Inverness mixed train at Corriemuillie Summit, near Garve in June 1967. *Roy M.B. Crombie/SRPS*

#486 BR Type 2 Bo-Bo D.E. #D5131 splutters over the summit of Ravens Rock with a Kyle of Lochalsh to Inverness mixed train in June 1967. *Roy M.B. Crombie/SRPS*

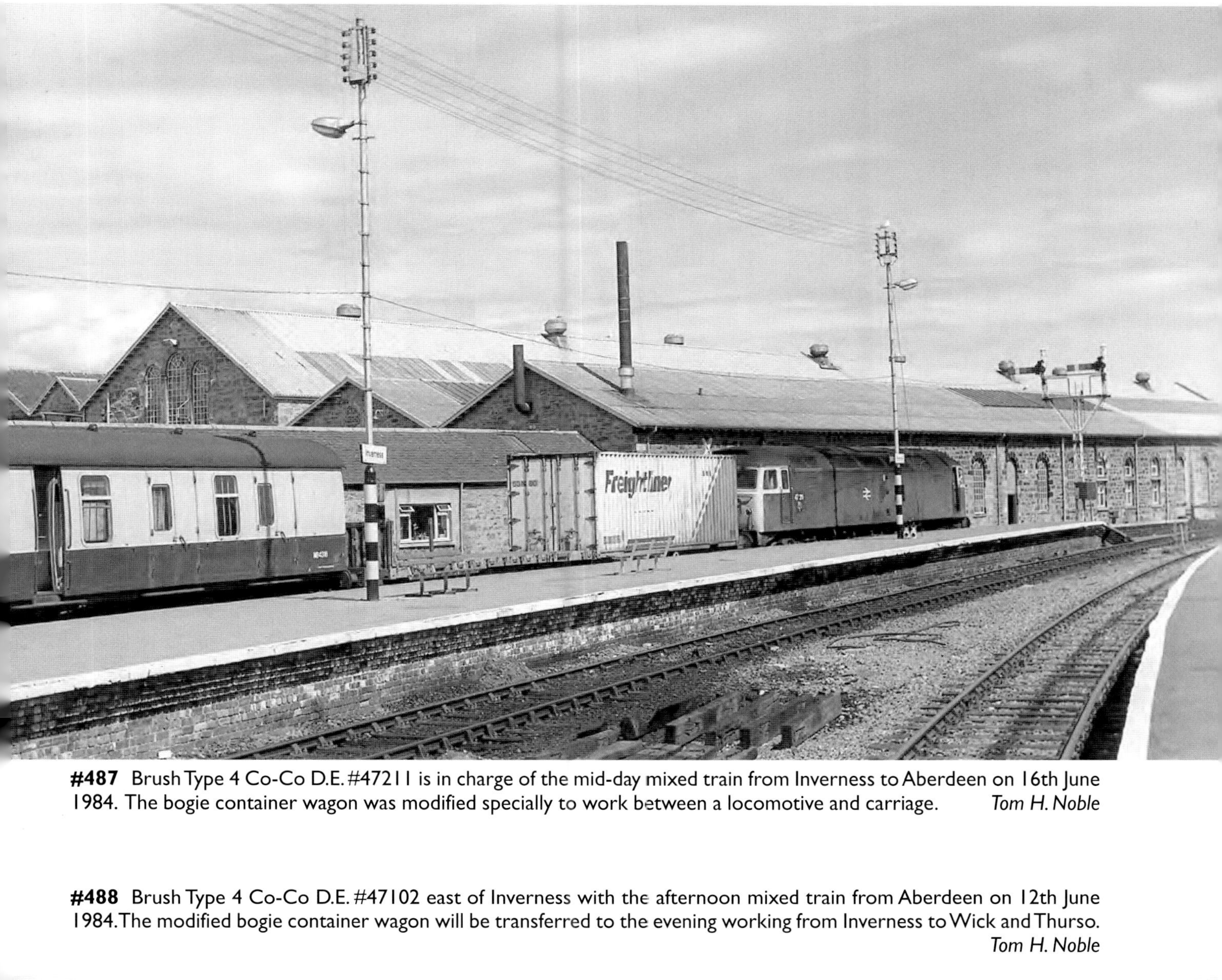

#487 Brush Type 4 Co-Co D.E. #47211 is in charge of the mid-day mixed train from Inverness to Aberdeen on 16th June 1984. The bogie container wagon was modified specially to work between a locomotive and carriage. *Tom H. Noble*

#488 Brush Type 4 Co-Co D.E. #47102 east of Inverness with the afternoon mixed train from Aberdeen on 12th June 1984. The modified bogie container wagon will be transferred to the evening working from Inverness to Wick and Thurso. *Tom H. Noble*

#489 BRCW Type 2 Bo-Bo D.E. #27005 makes a smoky departure from Keith Junction with the morning mixed train from Inverness to Aberdeen on 22nd May 1980. The practice of coupling regular examples of the fast diminishing fleet of Blue Spot insul fish vans next to the locomotive soon resulted in those formerly white or ice blue painted vans being weathered very quickly. This was due to the vans being subjected to the double adhesion of locomotive engine exhaust, and locomotive, van and train coach brake shoe abrasion, plus other dirt all being applied at speed. *Geo. C. O'Hara*

#490 A brace of BRCW Type 2 Bo-Bo D.E.s #26040 and #26041 double head a mixed train from Aberdeen to Inverness away from a snow covered Gartly in January 1982. *Sandy Murdoch/TTT*

#491 BRCW Type 2 Bo-Bo D.E. #27007 is panned travelling at least 60 mph in charge of the morning Inverness to Aberdeen mixed train near Hatton of Fintray, where the River Don meanders in the background, on 1st May 1980.
Geo. C. O'Hara

#492 An unusual truly mixed train in the consist of BR Swindon 3-car DMU (partly obscured by the lineside shrubs and trees), Gloucester R.C. & W. Co. single railcar, and Blue Spot insul fish van is seen on an Inverness to Aberdeen service west of Dyce on 29th June 1979. *Geo. C. O'Hara*

#493 NBL Type 2 Bo-Bo D.E. #D6143 in charge of a mixed train to Elgin about to leave Lossiemouth during March 1963, where insul fish vans and 12-ton vanfits make up the goods wagon element of the working. *Norris Forrest/TTT*

#494 Unidentified EE Type 1 Bo-Bo D.E.in charge of a mixed train to Elgin at Lossiemouth in September, 1963. *G.N.Turnbull*

#495 NBL Type 2 Bo-Bo D.E. #D6141 runs round its mixed train consist at Lossiemouth on the 4th April 1964, (the last day of passenger services on the branch to the Morayshire fishing village). On this occasion the mixed content of the train working from Elgin, was a far travelled ex Southern Railway 12-ton vanfit. *Roy Hamilton*

#496 A pair of BRCW Type 2 Bo-Bo D.E.s #D5345 and D5331 approach Pitlochry with the afternoon mixed train from Inverness to Edinburgh Waverley and Glasgow Buchanan Street on 24th June 1961. This lengthy train would be divided into its respective destination sections at Perth.
WAC Smith/TTT

#497 Ballinluig Junction on 9th January 1965, with BRCW Type 2 Bo-Bo D.E. #D5324 about to leave with the mid morning mixed train for Aberfeldy, containing in addition to an ex LMSR corridor brake coach, three 13-ton highfits and three 16-ton minfit wagons plus a brake van. *Douglas Hume*

#498 Aberfeldy in January 1965, with BRCW Type 2 Bo-Bo D.E. #D5336 just having arrived with a mixed train from Ballinluig Junction. *Norris Forrest/TTT*

#499 BRCW Type 2 D.E. #D5363 seen west of Corpach with a long mixed train consist of more wagons than the single ex-LNER passenger brake coach from Mallaig to Fort William, passing the side of Loch Eil in June 1962.

Roy M.B. Crombie/SRPS

#500 Unidentified BRCW Type 2 Bo-Bo D.E. in charge of a mixed train formation from Mallaig to Fort William in the summer of 1968, where the vehicle at the rear of the working is a 12-ton vanfit, as the conveyance of fish traffic by rail had just recently been withdrawn. *Norris Forrest/TTT*

#501 The loco crew of NBL Type 2 Bo-Bo D.E. #D6157 make their way to the station bothy for a welcome brew before taking out the morning mixed train from Peterhead to Aberdeen, via a join-up at Maud Junction with the same working from Fraserburgh in the summer of 1965. Note how the Blue Spot insul fish van identification number has been scrubbed clean of grime. *Sandy Murdoch/TTT*

#502 BRCW Type 2 Bo-Bo D.E. #D5355 sweeps into the island platform at Connel Ferry with the mid-day mixed train from Oban to Glasgow Buchanan Street conveying two Blue Spot insul fish vans at the rear on 12th May 1962. *Roy Hamilton*

#503 BRCW Type 2 Bo-Bo D.E. #D5303 breasts Borthwick Bank on the former Waverley Route with an afternoon mixed train from Edinburgh Waverley to Carlisle on 11th May 1963. The two Blue Spot insul fish vans behind the locomotive have travelled from one of the rail connected fishing ports in the Scottish Region. *WAC Smith/TTT*

#504 The lonely signal box at Whitrope Summit, and the photographer's Triumph Herald car provide part of the background as BRCW Type 2 Bo-Bo D.E. #D5313 prepare to descend towards Edinburgh Waverley with a mixed train from Carlisle conveying a few vanfits coupled to the last carriage in August 1966. *Roy M.B. Crombie/SRPS*

#505 EE Type 4 Co-Co D.E. #D408 near Dalmeny with a Perth to Edinburgh Waverley mixed working in July 1970. Note the three impressive girder towers of the Forth Bridge just beyond the distant tree line.

John M. Boyes – The Armstrong Railway Photographic Trust

#506 The Perth to London Kensington Olympia Motorail (mixed) train passes Greenfoot headed by EE Type 4 Co-Co D.E. #D403 in June 1973. Note the inclusion of BR Mk1 'Sleepers' in the formation of passenger coaches.

Morrison Bryce

#507 EE Type 4 1Co-Co1 D.E. #D256 near Joppa with the afternoon mixed stopping train from Edinburgh Waverley to Newcastle on 23rd April 1961, conveying three Blue Spot insul fish vans from some rail connected Scottish sea port.
Ken Falconer

#508 Not a true mixed train in the sense that there are no passenger coaches in the consist (only passenger brake vans), as an unidentified EE Type 4 1Co-Co1 D.E. rumbles downhill from Dalrymple Junction with a mixed parcels and vehicles working from Carlisle to Stranraer on 23rd February 1979. *Geo. C. O'Hara*

Section 9
Goods Depots & Marshalling Yards

At the formation of B.R. in 1948 the infant nationalised British Railways system inherited several hundred goods depots in Scotland, virtually all of which adjoined passenger stations, usually all with the same name. In addition to these basic goods stations, all of the large Scottish towns and cities inherited many large specifically constructed goods and mineral depots which handled the vast volume of railborne goods traffic which was the modus operandi in G.B. before the construction of the motorway network. All of these large depots were located in the centre of these conurbations, and at the height of operation, were invariably full of several types of general merchandise vans and many different kinds of open and flat wagons. All large depots had mobile cranes along with road vans, lorries and mechanical horses in the era of British Railways. Railborne freight to and from these goods stations and depots remained constant until these facilities were financially scrutinised in Dr. Beeching's 1963 report, endorsement of which set in train the terminal decline of wagonload freight throughout Scotland, which took nearly three decades to accomplish.

The 1955 B.R. Modernisation Plan authorised the construction of several new marshalling yards in Scotland, along with the upgrading of all of the existing yards already in operation. This well intentioned investment quickly became a loss-making embarrassment. Incessant traffic flow contractions, the concurrent demise of traditional Scottish heavy engineering industries and the implementation of more efficient methods of freight train operations brought about primarily by the advent of more flexible types of diesel traction, all led to fewer amounts of wagons carrying lesser amounts of freight. Surprisingly, several rural lines which were denuded of their passenger train services in the implementation of the Beeching Report, retained freight services for many years thereafter, importing coal, cement, steel, fertiliser, fuel oil and general merchandise, and despatching mainly agricultural produce, fish and for a short time livestock.

LIST OF LOCATIONS ILLUSTRATED

509 THURSO
510 KYLE OF LOCHALSH
511 INVERNESS
512 LOSSIEMOUTH
513 ELGIN
514 FRASERBURGH
515 FRASERBURGH
516 FRASERBURGH
517 FRASERBURGH
518 MAUD JUNCTION
519 PETERHEAD
520 PETERHEAD
521 PETERHEAD
522 PETERHEAD
523 INVERURIE
524 ABERDEEN GUILD STREET
525 ABERDEEN GUILD STREET
526 ABERDEEN WATERLOO
527 KEITH JUNCTION
528 OLDMELDRUM
529 BALLATER
530 BRECHIN
531 BRECHIN
532 BRECHIN
533 MONTROSE EAST
534 FORFAR
535 ARBROATH
536 OBAN
537 OBAN
538 FORT WILLIAM
539 ABERFELDY
540 CRIEFF
541 THORNTON JUNCTION
542 CAMERON BRIDGE
543 COUPAR ANGUS
544 KIRKCALDY
545 ALLOA EAST
546 ALLOA NEW YARD
547 MILLERHILL
548 CURRIE
549 CURRIE
550 COLINTON
551 LEITH SOUTH
552 SCOTLAND STREET
553 GREENOCK
554 CLYDEBANK WEST
555 KILSYTH
556 GOVAN
557 HIGH STREET(GLASGOW)
558 DALMARNOCK
559 PARTICK CENTRAL
560 SCOTSTOUN WEST
561 WHITEINCH RIVERSIDE
562 YOKER
563 PINKSTON
564 AIRDRIE NORTH
565 EAST KILBRIDE
566 AIRDRIE EAST
567 FALKLAND YARD
568 AYR HARBOUR
569 AYR (OLD) GOODS
570 DUMFRIES

#509 BRCW Type 2 Bo-Bo D.E. #D5346 shunts a variety of four wheel vans and wagons in THURSO yard during July 1970, by which time the fleet of former British Railways road vehicles seen in the background, had obtained a new yellow livery and new ownership in the name of NCL. *Geo. C. O'Hara*

#510 Unidentified BR Type 2 Bo-Bo D.E. shunts a long rake of four-wheel vanfits into one of the goods reception sidings at KYLE OF LOCHALSH in August 1970. *Norris Forrest/TTT*

#511 Unidentified Brush Type 4 Co-Co D.E. leaves the crammed and extensive goods yard at INVERNESS with a lightweight Speedlink trip service to Invergordon on 5th May 1981. *Geo. C. O'Hara*

#512 Minus one blade of its buffer-mounted snow-plough, NBL Type 2 Bo-Bo D.E. #D6143 shunts several different types of insul fish vans at LOSSIEMOUTH goods yard during March 1963. *Norris Forrest/TTT*

#513 BR Type 2 Bo-Bo D.E. #25227 shunts a rake of air braked vans and wagons in the modernised Speedlink goods depot at ELGIN on 18th April 1978. Noticeable in the yard are two different and distinctive types of crane. The mobile straddle carrier is for the loading and unloading of containers, whereas the single jib mobile is to handle loose freight, like the girders on the pair of bogie bolster wagons behind the locomotive. *Geo. C. O'Hara*

#514 A panoramic view of FRASERBURGH goods yard and station on 21st September 1963. In addition to a 2-car Cravens DMU at the station, two unidentified NBL Type 2 Bo-Bo D.E.s can be seen amidst a sea of mainly Blue Spot insul fish vans, conflats, vanfits and mineral wagons in this formerly busy Scottish railway terminus. Missing from this scene are any fuel oil tank wagons which worked to the yard conveying mainly diesel for the ports large fishing fleet. *Douglas Hume*

#515 By 1970 FRASERBURGH goods yard ha contracted considerably, with several sidings lifted t reflect the reduction in fish traffic. In the last years of i existence an unidentified NBL Type 2 Bo-Bo D.E. shun part of a trip service from Aberdeen Craiginches yar The former loco shed and station buildings still rema intact, but minus their trackwork. *Jack Kernah*

#516 On 28th June 1977 BR Type 2 Bo-Bo D.E. #2502 shunts a short rake at FRASERBURGH goods yard. the consist are a former GWR Python parcels van ar two lowmac wagons, converted to convey insulated fi containers following the withdrawal of the fleet of Bl Spot insul fish vans. *Geo. C. O'Ha*

#517 FRASERBURGH yard on the pouring wet day January 29th 1979, nine months before the entire closu of the branch from Dyce. BRCW Type 2 Bo-Bo D #26029 sits at the head of the return working Aberdeen, as the former bustling goods yard prepares f future use as an industrial estate. *Geo. C. O'Ha*

#518 NBL type 2 Bo-Bo D.E. #D6140 shunts a rake of conflat wagons at a very busy looking MAUD JUNCTION goods yard during November 1964, where the single road goods shed at the end of the yard is still in use. *Norris Forrest/TTT*

#519 Unidentified BR Type 2 Bo-Bo D.E. shunts the goods yard at PETERHEAD in the spring of 1968. Note the fact that all signal arms have been removed from both signal posts following the withdrawal of the passenger service on the branch in 1965. *Keith G. Jones*

9
D8616

#522 BRCW Type 2 Bo-Bo D.E. #D5310 at PETERHEAD shunting a rake of vanfits at one of the former station platforms of the freight only Buchan town on 7th July 1969. *Jack Kernahan*

PREVIOUS PAGE:
#520 With the former GNSR two road engine shed at PETERHEAD seemingly in use as a rubbish dump, Clayton Type 1 Bo-Bo D.E. #D8616 shunts the still busy looking goods yard in April 1966. Closure of this yard in September 1970, a few years before the UK Offshore construction industry started in the North Sea was a rationalisation decision by the Board of BR in Scotland which baffled all who later worked in that industry, and were amazed at the thousands of subsequent lorry journeys thereafter made to and from the Buchan town. *Geo. C. O'Hara*

#521 NBL Type 2 Bo-Bo D.E. #D6139 leaves PETERHEAD yard with a rake of vanfits laden with produce from the nearby Crosse & Blackwell food processing plant on 23rd July 1963, whilst an unidentified sister locomotive waits at the station with a passenger service to Maud Junction. *Robin Nelson*

#523 Brush Type 4 Co-Co D.E. #47469 "Glasgow Chamber of Commerce" in the dated and abstract ScotRail livery shunts a train consisting of 2 molasses tanks and a lengthy rake of agricultural lime at INVERURIE on 1st June 1988. *Geo. C. O'Hara*

#524 BR 0-6-0 350 h.p. D.E. shunter #D3549 shunts a rake of vanfits and conflats at a busy ABERDEEN GUILD STREET goods yard on 22nd June 1960. *Ken Nuttall*

#525 BRCW Type 2 Bo-Bo D.E. #D5302 and an unidentified sister locomotive back onto a southbound express fish train consisting of Blue Spot insul fish vans at ABERDEEN GUILD STREET during a trial for the suitability of diesel traction on this once valued service in the summer of 1961. *Norris Forrest/TTT*

#526 EE 0-6-0 h.p. D.E. shunter #D3931 shunts some empty mineral wagons at ABERDEEN WATERLOO goods depot in July 1970. Note the tenements, some with bars on the windows in the background. *Geo. C. O'Hara*

#527 Andrew Barclay 0-4-0 204 h.p. D.M. shunter #D2416 shunts a rake of conflat wagons at KEITH JUNCTION goods yard on 21st June 1960. *Ken Nuttall*

#528 Andrew Barclay 0-4-0 204 h.p. D.M. shunter #D2414 and brake van at OLDMELDRUM goods yard in the summer of 1966, the last year of operation on the branch. *Sandy Murdoch/TTT*

#529 BALLATER station and goods yard on 23rd April 1962 with a Cravens 4-car DMU about to leave for Aberdeen, and an unidentified NBL Type 2 Bo-Bo D.E. sandwiched between two rakes of wagons at the goods shed siding. *Robin Nelson*

#530 BR Type 2 Bo-Bo D.E. #25244 brings a rake of brand new looking air-braked hopper wagons conveying agricultural lime from Coxhoe, North Eastern Region to BRECHIN east goods yard on 11th November 1980. *Geo. C. O'Hara*

#531 BRCW Type 2 Bo-Bo D.e. #26023 shunts a mixed rake of vanfits and empty mineral wagons at BRECHIN west goods yard on 17th November 1980, where the former passenger station looks amazingly vandal free nearly thirty years after the withdrawal of the passenger service on the branch. *Geo. C. O'Hara*

#532 BRCW Type 2 Bo-Bo D.E. #26008 appears to be emerging from the tiny cathedral at BRECHIN as it shunts the goods shed in the town on 22nd January 1979. This once busy Angus branch, reduced to freight only status for thirty years, closed completely in May 1981.

Geo. C. O'Hara

#533 MONTROSE EAST goods yard was still very busy with grain traffic, scrap metal and domestic coal when EE Type 1 Bo-Bo D.E. #D8028 visited with the Stephenson Locomotive Society/Branch Line Society Easter railtour on 22nd April 1964.

Roy Hamilton

#534 BRCW Type 2 Bo-Bo D.E. #27208 shunts vanfits and unfitted mineral wagons at FORFAR goods yard on 10th November 1980. Note the 'modernist' type signal box on the former station platform. This building remained as the goods office for the yardmaster up until the closure of the branch from Stanley Junction in the spring of 1982.

Geo. C. O'Hara

#535 Hunslet 0-6-0 204 h.p. D.M. shunter #D2584 positions vanfits and conflats at ARBROATH goods yard during January 1966. Note the covered coal yard, a typical feature in several Scottish goods yards.

Sandy Murdoch/TTT

#536 An unidentified BRCW Type 2 Bo-Bo D.E. can just be seen emerging from the engine shed as an ex LMS Ivatt 2-6-0 shunts the adjacent busy looking OBAN goods yard, and a pair of ex Caley McIntosh 0-4-4 tank locomotives await their fate in the yard headshunt siding on 12th May 1962. *Roy Hamilton*

#537 BRCW Type 2 Bo-Bo D.E. #27009 shunts a short goods train from Cadder Yard at OBAN station goods sidings on 27th April 1979. Note the selective isolation of the station signalling system in the run down towards closure of the signal box and the installation of state of the art electronic signalling on the line. *Geo. C. O'Hara*

#538 The new combined engine shed and goods yard at FORT WILLIAM on 10th July 1978, is passed by an unidentified BR Type 2 Bo-Bo D.E. hauling a rake of caustic soda liquor tanks from the nearby Corpach pulp and paper mill. *Geo. C. O'Hara*

#539 BR Type 2 Bo-Bo D.E. #D5123 accelerates past the recently closed goods yard and former freight depot at ABERFELDY with a one-coach 'railbus' service for Ballinluig Junction in the spring of 1965. Note the dilapidated state of the former engine shed on the left. *WAC Smith/TTT*

#540 The cleft of Glen Turret between the distant Perthshire hills provides the background to Clayton Type 1 Bo-Bo D.E. #D8571 at the extensive goods yard at CRIEFF with a trip freight for Perth new yard on 31st May 1967. *Sandy Smeaton*

#541 Part of the once extensive and now truncated yard at THORNTON JUNCTION in September 1982. Note one of the concrete winding cages of the former showpiece Rothes Colliery, which had closed in the early-1960's after a short, costly and troubled career. Unidentified BRCW Type 2 Bo-Bo D.E. and a similarly unrecognisable EE type 1 Bo-Bo D.E. locomotive can be seen in the yard. *Geo. C. O'Hara*

#542 EE Type 3 Co-Co D.E. #37374 shunts Grainflow and Scottish Malt Distillers Polybulks, and 4-wheel CO_2 wagons at CAMERON BRIDGE yard and sidings of the former Distillers Company Ltd. on 21st February 1989, where part of the long closed island platform of the former passenger station with the same name can be seen to the left. *Geo. C. O'Hara*

#543 The coal yard at COUPAR ANGUS forms the backdrop as BRCW Type 2 Bo-Bo D.E. #27039 trundles a rake of empty mineral wagons back to Perth new yard from Forfar on 2nd October 1978. Note how the former station platforms have become overgrown eleven years after the withdrawal of the passenger train service through Strathmore.
Geo. C. O'Hara

#544 Hunslet 0-6-0 204 h.p. D.M. shunter #D2584 is seen at KIRKCALDY goods yard on 3rd November 1960, where the adjacent architecture reflects the former prosperity of this famous Fife town which was built on the manufacture of linoleum. *Hamish Stevenson*

#545 NBL 0-4-0 225 h.p. D.H. shunter #D2744 "fly-shunts" a rake of four-wheel vans and wagons at ALLOA EAST during the mid-1960's.
Sandy Murdoch/TTT

#546 The driver and guard of EE Type 1 Bo-Bo D.E. #20111 pose for the camera prior to working a trip from ALLOA NEW YARD to the nearby Menstrie United Molasses Co. private siding on 20th January 1978. Note the miniscule bothy, brazier and privvy provided for the amenities of the railway workers. Note also in the distance, the rows of buffer stops at the end of what once were loops in the fast contracting marshalling yard. *Geo. C. O'Hara*

#547 BRCW Type 2 Bo-Bo D.E. #26006 departs from the vast marshalling yard at MILLERHILL with a MGR working to nearby Cockenzie power station on 16th April 1981. *Morrison Bryce*

PREVIOUS PAGE:

#548 NBL 0-4-0 225 h.p. D.H. shunter #D2754 works the goods yard at CURRIE during September 1960. *Norris Forrest/TTT*

#549 Three distinctive and different grades of domestic coal can be seen in the wagons being shunted by BR 0-6-0 350 h.p. D.E. shunter at an overgrown CURRIE goods yard during October 1967. *G.N.Turnbull*

#550 COLINTON goods yard being shunted by BR 0-6-0 350 h.p. D.E. shunter #D3888 on 15th May 1961. Note the newly installed concrete balustrade on the road bridge over the railway. *Robin Nelson*

#551 BR 0-6-0 350 h.p. D.E. shunter #08421 shunts a rake of imported coal in air braked MGR wagons at LEITH SOUTH goods yard on 29th May 1986. *Geo. C. O'Hara*

#552 SCOTLAND STREET goods yard is worked by NBL 0-4-0 225 h.p. D.H. shunter #D2750 during March 1962. *Norris Forrest/TTT*

#553 EE Type 1 Bo-Bo D.E.s #20192 and #20228 run round the Saturdays only container train from Coatbridge at the Clyde Port Authority terminal, GREENOCK on 5th July 1986. This facility was located on the site of the former GSWR terminus of Princes Pier. Note the smoke from a RN frigate undergoing builders trials in the Firth of Clyde. *Geo. C. O'Hara*

#554 Ex-works BR 0-6-0 350 h.p. D.E. shunter #08883 'positions' some 16-ton coal wagons at CLYDEBANK WEST goods and mineral station on 22nd July 1976. This yard closed completely on 4th October 1978, and was relocated to a new goods yard location at nearby Dalmuir Riverside. Note another example of a covered coal unloading facility in the background. *Geo. C. O'Hara*

PREVIOUS PAGE:

#555 EE Type 1 Bo-Bo D.E. #D8112 at KILSYTH goods yard with a trip freight working from Cadder Yard on 1st May 1964, where yet another example of a Scottish covered coal yard can be seen. *Roy Hamilton*

#556 Clayton Type 1 Bo-Bo D.E. #D8525 shunts a rake of mainly four-wheel plate wagons along with some bogie bolsters and boplate wagons all laden with steel plates and sections for the nearby Fairfield Shipbuilding & Eng. Co. Ltd., at GOVAN goods yard on 8th June 1966, by which time the goods shed had been abandoned and only steel, coal and scrap metal was handled at the location. *Hamish Stevenson*

#557 HIGH STREET goods depot in Glasgow in August 1976, when many different types of railway goods wagon can be seen being loaded and unloaded by mobile and gantry cranes, and an unidentified BR 0-6-0 350h.p. D.E. shunter is the sole type of traction. *Geo. C. O'Hara*

#558 A hybrid 4 car DMU headed by a Metro-Cammell 2 car unit emerges from Dalmarnock tunnel and passes the large and busy DALMARNOCK goods and mineral depot on 1st October 1964. The line in the centre led to Possil via Balornock, and rejoined the line on which the DMU is travelling at Partick West. *Roy Hamilton*

#559 BR 0-6-0 350 h.p. D.E. shunter brings a rake of 4-wheel tank wagons from the Esso terminal at Bowling via a trip working from Yoker yard to PARTICK CENTRAL goods yard where domestic fuel oil, household coal and scrap metal was still handled on 18th January 1978. *Geo. C. O'Hara*

#560 The goods yard at SCOTSTOUN WEST was the western junction for the Clydeside Tramway system of street running railways, built by the former Caledonian Railway to serve many shipyards, engine works, factories and foundries on the north bank of the River Clyde. Diesel traction has taken over in the summer of 1959 as a BR 0-6-0 350 h.p. D.E., and an NBL 0-4-0 225 h.p. D.H. shunter can be seen in different sidings, along with plate and boplate wagons. The famous shipyards of Yarrow & Co. Ltd., and the adjacent Blythswood Shipbuilding Co. Ltd. can be seen beyond the goods yard.

#561 Halfway along the Clydeside Tramway was located WHITEINCH RIVERSIDE goods and mineral depot. This once busy yard handled coal, scrap metal, steel, general merchandise, and grain and livestock in transit. In this winter 1959 view when the m.v. TREVAYLOR (6501 g.r.t.) has just been launched from the nearby shipyard of Barclay Curle & Co. Ltd., an unidentified NBL 0-4-0 225 h.p. D.H. shunter can just be seen beyond the boom tip of the shipyard 150 ton hammerhead crane whilst shunting in the snow covered goods yard. both photos: *Courtesy of Jim M. McIntosh*

#562 BR 0-6-0 350 h.p. D.E. shunter #08621 banks a trip freight headed by an unidentified BR Type 2 Bo-Bo D.E. out of YOKER yard bound for Cadder Yard in April 1976. Note the skyline crammed with the jibs of many cranes in some of the extant Glasgow shipyards. *Geo. C. O'Hara*

#563 EE Type 3 Co-Co D.E. #37039 shunts the extensive 'coal ree' sidings at PINKSTON goods and mineral depot on 19th April 1982. Note among the untidy layout of the scene, the common practice in west of Scotland coal yards to use empty oil drums as balusters for the storage of coal. *Tom H. Noble*

#564 BR 0-6-0 350 h.p. D.E. shunter #D3395 positions several mineral wagons at AIRDRIE NORTH goods and mineral depot on 11th April 1962. *Robin Nelson*

#565 EE Type 1 Bo-Bo D.E. #20108 shunts loaded and empty coal wagons at EAST KILBRIDE goods yard on 27th May 1974. *WAC Smith/TTT*

#566 Unidentified BR 0-6-0 350 h.p. D.E. shunter and brake van at AIRDRIE EAST goods depot on 9th May 1961. *Robin Nelson*

#567 EE Type 4 1Co-Co1 D.E. #40022 leaves part of the extensive FALKLAND YARD in Ayr with a trip working conveying cement for Irvine, and caustic soda liquor for the I.C.I. chemical plant at Ardeer on 29th November 1983.
Geo. C. O'Hara

#568 AYR HARBOUR goods yard on 27th November 1982 with BR 0-6-0 350 h.p. D.E. shunter #08446 marshalling a long rake of fitted gunpowder wagons for distribution to the I.C.I. Nobel Division rail connected explosives works at Bogside, Ardeer and Powfoot.
Geo. C. O'Hara

#569 AYR (OLD) GOODS depot in May 1972 not long before the site was closed and lifted. Unidentified BR 0-6-0 350h.p. D.E. shunter is marshalling the consist of a special train which will convey several military vehicles bound for British Army manoeuvres at Devizes in Wiltshire. *Derek Cross*

#570 BR Type 2 Bo-Bo D.E. #25230 at DUMFRIES goods and mineral depot on 12th July 1984. The locomotive is marshalling a hybrid consist of bogie bolster wagons, Speedlink TOPS coded wagons with OAA, and OTA identification acronyms in readiness to accept loads of harvested timber from the Galloway forests for delivery to Chirk in North Wales. The VBA and VDA vans in the sidings are for explosives traffic to nearby I.C.I. Powfoot works. *Geo. C. O'Hara*

Section 10

Trip Freight Workings & Private Sidings

The railway system in Britain was conceived to carry bulk raw materials from various sources of extraction to many places of manufacture, and thence to a network of warehouses, goods depots, docks and further locations throughout the entire country. This labyrinth of lines, yards and sidings was served by hundreds of slow-moving locomotives hauling and shunting thousands of mainly short-wheelbase four-wheel wagons under the category of "trip workings".

This practice, which was a throwback from the inception of the railway ethos, was still the major method of conveying raw materials and finished products throughout virtually the entire spectrum of Scottish manufacturing industry at the formation of British Railways in 1948. So intensive was the spread of private railway sidings that several main railway routes had parallel slow running and shunting lines built alongside to allow for this essential rail freight system to function.

In the city of Glasgow the famous Clydeside Tramway was built parallel to the adjacent double track formation from Glasgow Central Low Level, and ran for a distance of about three miles. This mainly street running system, the last remnants of which closed in 1978 once served five former shipyards, many factories, a granary, an animal lairage, several docks, three marine engine building works and had its own dedicated goods depot at Whiteinch Riverside yard. When the system was eventually worked by diesel shunters it still had a programme of multiple shift working over 6 days a week.

LIST OF LOCATIONS ILLUSTRATED

#571 Brush Type 4 Co-Co D.E. #47048 shunts the morning trip working from Inverness yard at the former British Aluminium Company Ltd., smelter sidings at Invergordon on 23rd May 1980. This plant, once seen as a source of many jobs in the eastern Highlands, closed in 1981. In its brief existence it generated considerable amounts of rail freight including: alumina, liquified petroleum gas and finished aluminium ingots. Needless to say when it was later dismantled its fabric removal was carried in many trainloads of scrap. *Geo. C. O'Hara*

#572 EE Type 4 1Co-Co1 D.E. #40158 powers the morning trip working from Inverness yard to Invergordon, north of Alness on 13th June 1980. This nicely mixed freight was convey ng cement for the MK Shand pipe coating yard, empty whisky containers for the Cutty Sark distillery and about a dozen covhops laden with alumina from Burntisland for the British Aluminium Co. Ltd. smelter. *Geo. C. O'Hara*

#573 EE Type 4 1Co-Co1 D.E. #40158 approaches Alness with the morning trip freight from Inverness yard to Invergordon on the hazy morning of 10th June 1980. In addition to several OBA wagons and covhops for the British Aluminium Co. Ltd., private siding, there are two bogie trestle wagons loaded with wide plates for the former oil platform construction yard of Highlands Fabricators Ltd at Nigg on the nearby Cromarty Firth. *Geo. C. O'Hara*

#574 EE Type 4 1Co-Co1 D.E. #40103 slowly hauls a rake of empty vacuum-fitted 35-ton bulk grain wagons away from the Distillers Company Ltd maltings plant at Burghead bound for Doncaster Belmont yard on 28th June 1977.
Geo. C. O'Hara

#575 EE Type 4 1Co-Co1 D.E. #40168 is seen south of Keith with a trip working to the Associated British Maltsters Ltd. siding and grain silo at Dufftown on 28th June 1977. Also in the train consist is a single 16-ton mineral wagon loaded with domestic coal.
Geo. C. O'Hara

5849

PREVIOUS PAGE:
#576 The driver of EE Type I Bo-Bo D.E. #D8031 manages a wee smile for the photographer as he prepares to shunt the daily trip goods from Craigellachie at Dailuaine Distillery private siding on Speyside on 30th June 1966. Note how attractive the rake of 35-ton vacuum-fitted grain wagons look adorned with individual colourful logo bedecked hoardings depicting different brands of Distillers Company Limited Scotch whisky.
John M. Boyes/ The Armstrong Railway Photographic Trust

#577 Looking almost brand new EE Type I Bo-Bo D.E. #D8028 prepares to leave the long closed but still intact and unvandalised station at Alford with the return trip working to Kittybrewster in October 1964. *GNSRA archives*

#578 Unidentified Andrew Barclay 0-4-0 204 h.p. D.M. shunter propels a rake of conflat wagons loaded with what looks like insulated meat containers at Lethenty in the early 1960's, while working the trip freight service on the short branch from Inverurie to Oldmeldrum. *Norris Forrest/TTT*

#579 Andrew Barclay 0-4-0 204 h.p. D.M. shunter #D2424 leaves the York Street steel stockyard siding of the former shipyard of Hall Russell Ltd., in Aberdeen during March 1961. The locomotive has just shunted a few plate wagons and is returning along the cobbled dockside tramway to Waterloo Goods yard. The ship in the background was the stylish M.V. LETITIA, 4381 g.r.t., built by the yard for the Donaldson Line Ltd of Glasgow, and plied the North Atlantic for many years. *Norris Forrest/TTT*

#580 Ex-works BR 0-6-0 350 h.p. D.E. shunter #08719 leaves Waterloo Goods yard and begins the gentle climb to the junction at Kittybrewster with two empty china clay slurry wagons for Craiginches yard on 24th April 1985.
Geo. C. O'Hara

#581 Brush Type 4 Co-Co D.E. #47413 rushes a trip freight from Craiginches yard to Inverurie past the site of the former yard and loco shed at Kittybrewster on 17th May 1988. The train is conveying calcium carbonate for the paper mill in the town, as well as a few hundred tons of agricultural lime for Aberdeenshire farmers. *Geo. C. O'Hara*

#582 BR Type 2 Bo-Bo D.E. #25072 between Bridge of Dun and Kinnaber Junction with a lightweight trip freight from Brechin to Montrose on 2nd October 1978. Note the prime concrete track, a relic of when the line was the main route from Aberdeen to Perth. *Geo. C. O'Hara*

#583 BRCW Type 2 Bo-Bo D.E. #26043 arrives at Montrose on 10th October 1989 with a trip working from Dundee conveying three bogie agricultural lime wagons.
Tom H. Noble

#584 Andrew Barclay 0-4-0 204 h.p. D.M. shunter #D2415 propels a rake of four wheel unfitted bitumen tank wagons into the Wm. Briggs tar refinery siding off the Dundee harbour railway system near Camperdown Junction during January 1966. *Norris Forrest/TTT*

#585 Hunslet 0-6-0 204 h.p. D.M. shunter #D2575 trundles a trip freight from St. Andrews to Leuchars Junction past Guardbridge signal box on 28th April 1967. *Hamish Stevenson*

#586 EE Type 1 Bo-Bo D.E. #20202 brings a trip freight conveying a load of imported paper pulp from Methil Dock bound for Thornton Junction past the siding to Methil power station on 30th July 1985. Note the former LMSR brake van at the rear of the train, a rare sight in the 1980s. *Geo. C. O'Hara*

#587 EE Type 1 Bo-Bo D.E.s #20218 and #20211 take a lengthy trip freight of loaded MDV coal wagons from Westfield open cast site past the scarred Fife landscape for Thornton Junction yard on 30th July 1985. *Geo. C. O'Hara*

#588 The extinct volcanic cusp of the Largo Law (952 ft) provides the backdrop to BRCW Type 2 Bo-Bo D.E. #26024 in charge of a short trip freight of three TTA tank wagons from Thornton Junction yard bound for the Distillers Company Limited plant at Cameron Bridge, where they will be loaded with CO^2, on 23rd November 1988. *Geo. C. O'Hara*

PREVIOUS PAGE:
#589 EE Type 3 Co-Co D.E. #D6846 propels a trip freight working from Thornton Junction yard towards the terminus of the short Crombie branch on 4th April 1967. *Hamish Stevenson*

#590 Andrew Barclay 0-4-0 204 h.p. D.M. shunter #D2442 runs light engine with a brake van on a trip working from Kirkcaldy yard to shunt the grain silos on the harbour branch of the Fife town on 10th September 1970. *W.S. Sellar*

#591 BR 0-6-0 350 h.p. D.E. shunter #08515 hauls a nicely mixed Speedlink air-braked trip freight from the paper mills on the Auchmuty branch back to Thornton Junction yard on 5th September 1985. *Geo. C. O'Hara*

#592 The loco crew of (recently repainted in BR rail blue livery) Clayton Type 1 Bo-Bo D.E. #D8583 pose for the photographer whilst working a trip freight from Haddington to Millerhill yard on 18th September 1967. *G.N.Turnbull*

#593 EE Type 3 Co-Co D.E. #37108 takes a trip freight past the coal yard, sidings, carcass of the former engine shed and a couple of ex-mining spoil bings now all relics of the former industrial legacy of Bathgate, on 2nd April 1980.
Morrison Bryce

UM243

PREVIOUS PAGE:

#594 BR 0-6-0 350 h.p. D.E. shunter #D3542 nears Innerpeffrey and trundles through the flat and fertile Perthshire farming countryside with a trip goods working from Perth yard to Crieff on 11th August 1967. *Sandy Smeaton*

#595 EE Type 1 Bo-Bo D.E. #20216 hauls a short trip freight working consisting of four empty molasses tank wagons and a brake van from Menstrie to Alloa yard near Cambus Junction on 11th June 1979. *Geo. C. O'Hara*

#596 BR 0-6-0 350 h.p. D.M. shunter #08505 with a lengthy rake of empty OBA wagons from the British Aluminium Coy works at Bainsford being tripped to Grangemouth yard on the hazy and frosty morning of 28th March 1980. *Geo. C. O'Hara*

#597 The bothy at a snow covered Alloa yard helps to frame EE Type 1 Bo-Bo D.E. #20111 and a short train of two attractively painted maroon and navy United Molasses Co. Ltd. tank wagons and a brake van which have just worked a trip freight from Menstrie on 20th January 1978. *Geo. C. O'Hara*

#598 The Trossachs peak of Ben Ledi (2882 ft) can be seen in the distance as BRCW Type 2 Bo-Bo D.E. #26014 arrives at Cambus Junction to shunt the adjacent Distillers Company Ltd. maltings, with a trip freight from Grangemouth yard on 10th July 1987. Note the branch to Menstrie veering off to the right of the middle signal, where the four class B molasses tank wagons are destined. *Geo. C. O'Hara*

#599 The Touch Hills, to the left, William Wallace Monument and sluggish River Devon set the scene for BRCW Type 2 Bo-Bo D.E. #26014 (since preserved) hauling a trip freight from Menstrie to Alloa yard on 10th January 1986.

Geo. C. O'Hara

#600 Perhaps the most famous and iconic historical edifice in Scotland, the William Wallace Monument looks down on BRCW Type 2 Bo-Bo D.E. #26043 as it slows down to cross the ungated automatic level crossing at Causewayhead with a trip freight from Menstrie to Grangemouth yard on 15th January 1990.

Tom H. Noble

#601 Mist shrouds the top of Ben Cruachan (3695 ft) as BRCW Type 2 Bo-Bo D.E. #27009 shunts an engineers trip working at Taynuilt on 27th April 1979. Note the engineers ballast wagons in one of the sidings, which have been loaded with granite from the nearby Bonawe quarry. *Geo. C. O'Hara*

#602 The featureless background near Dumbarton Muir cannot detract from the rarity of BR 0-6-0 350 h.p. D.E. shunter #D3534 seen approaching Croftamie on 15th October 1958, with a trip goods working conveying two wagons of domestic coal from Balloch bound for Drymen, which was by then the end of the former Forth and Clyde junction route which formerly ran to Stirling. *Roy M.B. Crombie/SRPS*

#603 EE Type 1 Bo-Bo D.E. #20202 slows down to negotiate one of the gated level crossings on the branch from Polmaise Colliery, Fallin, Stirlingshire, as it trundles a trip MGR working to Longannet power station on the north bank of the River Forth, on 17th January 1979. *Geo. C. O'Hara*

#604 EE Type 1 Bo-Bo D.E. #20125 propels three bogie bolster wagons loaded with pipes for the BSC Imperial Tube works in Airdrie on a trip freight from BSC Clydesdale Tube works at nearby Mossend, on the truncated Calder branch during March 1985. *Geo. C. O'Hara*

#605 BR 0-6-0 350 h.p. D.E. shunter #08720 passes the Atlas scrapyard and metal recovery works in Airdrie with a trip freight from the nearby Moffat Mills branch on 3rd September 1974. The location of the brake van in the middle of the consist indicates several shunting operations were necessary on this working. *WAC Smith/TTT*

#606 EE Type 1 Bo-Bo D.E. #20099 propels a trip working consisting of several loaded MDV 21-ton higher capacity mineral wagons from Bedlay Colliery exchange sidings bound for Mossend yard on 9th December 1981. Note the plume of smoke from one of the pit pugs in front of the coal bing in the distance. *Tom H. Noble*

4

8Z02

PREVIOUS PAGE:
#607 Clayton Type 1 Bo-Bo D.E.s #D8530 and #D8537 work a trip freight consisting of what looks like a rake of British Steel Corporation internal user wagons, between the BSC Ravenscraig and Gartcosh steel mills on 8th July 1963.
W.S. Sellar

#608 Unidentified Clayton Type 1 Bo-Bo D.E. makes up its train at East Kilbride goods yard before working a trip freight back to Glasgow on 9th August 1963, long before the surrounding fields were developed with many houses and flats.
Robin Nelson

#609 Depicting a special train reporting number, EE Type 1 Bo-Bo D.E. #D8121 pulls a trip working from the Parkhead works of Sir William Arrol and Co. Ltd on to the short London Road goods branch on 1st July, 1965. *W.S. Sellar*

#610 NBL 0-4-0 225 h.p. D.H. shunter #D2737 works a trip working from Scotstoun West yard at Kelvin Hall on a foggy November day in 1960, note the silhouette of Glasgow University spire in the distance to the left.
Roy M.B. Crombie/SRPS

#611 BR 0-6-0 350 h.p. D.E. shunter #08733 and an unidentified sister loco perform trip (shunting) activities at the former General Terminus Quay and the adjacent reception sidings on 19th April 1978. This railhead in the heart of Glasgow was quickly closed and dismantled after the opening of the new BSC deep water port at Hunterston in the early 1980s.
Geo. C. O'Hara

#612 BR 0-6-0 350 h.p. D.E shunter #08621 trundles two rus begrimed laden unfitted bulk grai wagons from Meadowside granar bound for the Hiram Walke distillery at Dumbarton via Yoke yard during April 1976.

Geo. C. O'Har

#613 NBL 0-4-0 225 h.p. D.H shunter #D2735 on the Clydesid Tramway system with a trip freigh from Scotstoun West yard t Meadowside granary durin September 1963. The train i passing beneath the forme Whiteinch Riverside station, alon the Glasgow thoroughfare calle South Street. Note the recen erection of some galvanised ste fencing between the pavement an the street running railway.

Roy M.B. Crombie/SRP

#614 The driver of Andrew Barclay 0-4-0 204 h.p. D.M. shunter #D2432 raises a smile for the photographer as he crawls his short trip freight along South Street in the Whiteinch district of Glasgow on 24th November 1968. Passing an iconic Albion Atlantean double decker bus in the colours of Glasgow Corporation Transport, this working was the last train to operate on the street running section of the Clydeside Tramway. The short freight was hauling empty plate and boplate wagons from the nearby shipyard of the Scotstoun Division of Upper Clyde Shipbuilders Ltd, thus clearing the shipyard stockyard siding of all B.R. rolling stock. *W.S. Sellar*

#615 Unidentified EE Type 1 Bo-Bo D.E. takes a rake of vacuum fitted mineral wagons loaded with steel scrap from the Dalmuir shipbreaking yard of W.H. Arnott Young Ltd over the short chord from Anniesland to Maryhill Park, near Temple, with a trip freight from Yoker yard to Cadder yard on 11th April 1980. *Geo. C. O'Hara*

#616 The imposing skyline of tall cranes in the shipyard of Govan Shipbuilders Ltd provide a striking backdrop for BR 0-6-0 350 h.p. D.E. shunter #08719 hauling a dozen empty fuel oil tank wagons from Partick Central on a trip working to Yoker yard in January 1978. The train has just crossed over Whiteinch viaduct, where the arches beneath were rented to several small businesses. *Geo. C. O'Hara*

#617 BR 0-6-0 350 h.p. D.E. shunter #08718 passes the former Barclay Curle & Co. Ltd. marine engine works, and Scotstoun Marine shipyard of British Shipbuilders Ltd, with a mixed trip freight from Meadowside granary and Partick Central goods depot bound for Yoker yard in April 1976. The space between the railway embankment and the shipyard beyond used to contain the former Whiteinch Riverside goods yard. *Geo. C. O'Hara*

30
N133

JOHN BROWN

PREVIOUS PAGE:
#618 BR 0-6-0 350 h.p. D.E. shunter #08173 trundles past the closed, razed and overgrown site of Whiteinch Riverside station with a lengthy mixed trip of wagons from Meadowside granary and Partick Central to Yoker yard on a murky morning in March 1976. *Geo. C. O'Hara*

#619 BR 0-6-0 h.p. D.E. shunter #D3213 comes off the short branch to the former world famous Clydebank shipyard of John Brown & Co. Ltd., at Dalmuir Riverside with N.133 a trip working from Yoker yard on 20th December 1966. *Hamish Stevenson*

#620 The rapidly contracting, but still vast marshalling yard that was Rothesay Dock is passed by BR 0-6-0 350 h.p. D.E. shunter #08621 as it hauls a lengthy trip working conveying a trainload of imported coking coal up to Yoker yard in March 1976. In the distance are the cranes of the Marathon Le Tourneau jack-up drill rig yard (formerly John Brown & Co. (Clydebank) Ltd.), the renowned shipbuilding and engineering company. The nearer sheds and tarpaulin clad buildings are the site of the short lived offshore module construction yard of JBE Offshore Ltd., which built several modules and specialist structures for different platforms in the North Sea. *Geo. C. O'Hara*

#621 BR 0-6-0 350 h.p. D.E. shunter #08741 scoots past the site of the former Clydebank Riverside station, and the skyline depicting a plethora of shipyard hammerhead cranes, with the morning trip working from Yoker yard to Dalmuir in September 1976, conveying bulk whisky from Keith Junction bound for Chivas Bros. Ltd., and also a few empty mineral wagons for the W.H. Arnott Young shipbreaking yard. *Geo. C. O'Hara*

#622 A Greek bulk carrier with an unpronounceable name is unloaded at Rothesay Dock on 15th August 1979. Alongside BR 0-6-0 350 h.p. D.E. shunter #08853 prepares to haul a trip working up the short distance to Yoker yard with a rake of BSC bogie tippler wagons loaded with imported coking coal for BSC Ravenscraig steelworks. *Geo. C. O'Hara*

#623 BR Type 2 Bo-Bo D.E. #25269 waits for signal clearance at the site of the former Greenock Ladyburn locomotive shed, prior to reversing and crossing over to the James Watt Dock branch with a trip freight of molasses tank wagons from Mossend yard on 4th January 1985. *Geo. C. O'Hara*

#624 EE Type 3 Co-Co D.E. #37263 hauls a short trip freight comprising four molasses tank wagons away from the James Watt Dock tank farm of United Molasses Ltd bound for Menstrie via Mossend yard on 23rd October 1987. Moored alongside the adjacent Inchgreen quay is the self-propelled dynamically positioned semi-submersible drilling rig OCEAN ALLIANCE. Launched by the Scott-Lithgow Glen shipyard of British Shipbuilders Ltd in 1986, this vessel was, at the time of her launching, the largest such craft in the world, and was to be the last newbuild order completed by the renowned Port Glasgow shipyard. *Geo. C. O'Hara*

#625 EE Type 1 Bo-Bo D.E.s #20201 and #20228 cross over the main line to Hunterston and Largs with a trip freight working from Ayr Falkland yard to ICI Misk siding (seen on the extreme right), on 29th October 1985. This working will trip the three covered hopper wagons conveying rock salt to Dalry before returning to Ayr, with the four empty caustic soda liquor tanks. *Geo. C. O'Hara*

#626 Heavyweight locomotive power for a featherweight trip freight working as EE Type 3 Co-Co D.E. #37056 hauls a single VEA van from Giffen to Mossend yard on 7th September 1984. Note the overbridge in the distance marking the course of the former Caledonian Railway line to Kilwinning. *Geo. C. O'Hara*

#627 BRCW Type 2 Bo-Bo D.E. #26031 in bland grey Railfreight livery propels a rake of Cargowaggon bogie vans into the Hill Street siding of the Johnny Walker bottling plant at Kilmarnock on 13th November 1987. This working was a trip freight from Ayr Falkland yard. The empty wagons would be loaded with cases of Scotch whisky to be exported by rail to Europe. *Geo. C. O'Hara*

#628 EE Type 3 Co-Co D.E. #37156 has just propelled a rake of UKF PWA bogie fertiliser wagons off the morning trip working from Mossend yard into the UK Fertilisers Ltd. private siding at Lugton, as a Pressed Steel Coy. Ltd. Derby 3-car DMU set #387 passes on a service from Glasgow Central to Kilmarnock on 21st June 1985. *Geo. C. O'Hara*

#629 EE Type 1 Bo-BO D.E. #20036 shunts a variety of vacuum-fitted wagons in the yard of the former BSC Glengarnock steelworks on 4th April 1981. The four plate wagons in the foreground conveying steel billets to be rolled into special sections, at the steelworks had been tripped from Mossend yard earlier that day. *Geo. C. O'Hara*

#630 BRCW Type 2 Bo-Bo D.E. #26043 leaves the loop at Kilwinning with a trip working from Ayr Falkland yard to the Roche chemical works at Dalry on 7th May 1988. *Geo. C. O'Hara*

#631 BR 0-6-0 350 h.p. D.E. shunter #08344 'trips' a mixed rake of mainly steel carrying wagons from Ardrossan yard to the adjacent harbour on 12th June 1981. At this time Ardrossan yard had a couple of shunting locomotives stabled there. These locomotives were required to work the still operational harbour, as well as handle traffic to the nearby I.C.I. factories, the coal yard, and the Shell bitumen refiniery. *Geo. C. O'Hara*

#632 The former Shell bitumen refinery at Ardrossan is the backdrop for BR 0-6-0 350 h.p. D.E. shunter #08344 trip working a single bitumen tank wagon and 16-ton coal wagon from the yard, on 12th June 1981. Just visible to the right is Andrew Barclay 0-4-0 Fireless shunter, so designed for working in refineries. *Geo. C. O'Hara*

D6856

PREVIOUS PAGE:

#633 EE Type 3 Co-Co D.E. #D6856 with a trip working of empty mineral wagons for Cairnhill mine from Ayr Harbour in May 1969. In the foreground is the solum of the former railway line to Muirkirk, with beyond the denuded junction signal arms and chimney breast of the recently closed and demolished former signal box, which controlled the Gasswater branch to Cairnhill Mine. *Norris Forrest/TTT*

#634 The early morning mist in the upper Nith Valley provides soft mono-chrome tones as EE Type 1 Bo-Bo D.E.s 20193 and #20199 clatter a rake of laden MGR coal hoppers from Knockshinnoch with a trip working to Ayr Harbour during October 1985. *Geo. C. O'Hara*

#635 The site of the former Holehouse Junction veering off to the right is passed by EE Type 1 Bo-Bo D.E.s #20189 and #20145 hauling a trip working of empty HTV hoppers from Falkland yard to Waterside on 29th March 1985. *Geo. C. O'Hara*

#636 BR Type 2 Bo-Bo D.E. #25244 leaves the seemingly derelict landscape around the former NCB coal washing facility at Waterside with a trip working for Ayr harbour consisting of loaded HBA hoppers on 23rd February 1982. *Geo. C. O'Hara*

#637 BRCW Type 2 Bo-Bo D.E. #26031 crawls through the vegetation surrounding the Bogside branch with a trip working from Ayr Falkland yard on 22nd August, 1987. *Geo. C. O'Hara*

#638 BRCW Type 2 Bo-Bo D.E. #26037 leaves Ayr harbour with a trip working to Falkland yard, on 25th July 1987. The train is conveying a rake of air-braked Cemflo wagons loaded with imported Greek cement bound for Viewpark near Uddingston. *Geo. C. O'Hara*

#639 Recently out-shopped and re-painted BRCW Type 2 Bo-Bo D.E. #26029 leaves Dumfries yard with a trip working to the former ICI Powfoot explosives establishment on 6th September 1984. *Geo. C. O'Hara*

#641 Unidentified BR 0-6-0 350 h.p. D.E. shunter passes Maxton station signal box and level crossing with a trip freight from St. Boswells during July 1963.
Roy M.B. Crombie/SRPS

#640 The mist covered top of Criffel (1868 ft) provides the backdrop to BRCW Type 2 Bo-Bo D.E. #26038 hauling a trip freight comprising five fuel oil tank wagons from Dumfries to ICI Cargenbridge on 25th November 1987.
Geo. C. O'Hara

#642 BR 0-6-0 350 h.p. D.E. shunter #D3582 leaves St. Boswells with a mixed trip freight working for Kelso in July 1962. Note the indentations in the solum where the adjacent track has been lifted.
Roy Hamilton

Section 11

Specials & Rarities

This section of the book attempts to illustrate a few photographs depicting examples of the following types of railway operations, i.e. engineering, including track replacement and civil engineering, special workings, and special railtours for the interest of railway enthusiasts which were very common on former branch lines prior to their total closure. Invariably some of these tasks were unplanned, whilst the others were planned weeks in advance. Track possessions by breakdown crews sometimes closed routes entirely, or maybe allowed concurrent single line operation depending on the nature of the work being undertaken.

Engineering and breakdown trains sometimes consisted of two locomotives, with one at each end of the train, along with a rail-mounted crane, a tools and messing coach, spoil recovery, ballast and different types of flat wagons. These workings were not regular sightings on the Scottish permanent way with most planned engineering works schedules to be implemented during the night or over Sundays. Likewise was the transit of locomotives built by the former North British Locomotive Co. Ltd. at Glasgow for the Western and Eastern Regions of B.R., along with rolling stock made by the former Pressed Steel Co. Ltd. at Linwood, also for different regions of B.R. Several other types of locomotives and DMU's only ventured into Scotland on a very infrequent basis. This section contains several views of some of the above rarities and special workings on the former Scottish Region of BR.

The unique and oft derided phenomenon of railtours, germinated from the intimation of closure of the plethora of especially branch lines throughout the late 1960's on the Scottish Region of B.R. Initiated by mainly enthusiastic railway employees, these popular excursions soon acquired the endorsement and approval of senior railway management and became regular expeditions for many enthusiasts. Many if not all of the lines in Scotland which then existed were visited by railtour special trains, usually on a Saturday, and remarkably nearly all of these workings were sold out before departure. Initially steam traction was provided to haul these trains, but as steam replenishment facilities were gradually removed throughout the Scottish Region, then diesel locomotive or DMU haulage was later provided.

These B.R. approved railtours created perhaps the only opportunities for railwaymen and enthusiasts to take photographs of these lines, branches and stations, with an actual train sometimes showing revenue or stored wagons in sidings, before the locations visited were later closed.

LIST OF LOCATIONS ILLUSTRATED

643 TURRIFF
644 OLDMELDRUM
645 PETERHEAD
646 ABERDEEN FERRYHILL
647 ABERDEEN DOCKS
648 MALLAIG
649 TYNDRUM
650 CRIANLARICH
651 METHVEN
652 CRIEFF
653 KIRRIEMUIR
654 ST.ANDREWS
655 THROSK
656 STIRLING
657 DENNY
658 TORRANCE
659 COWLAIRS
660 SHIELDS JUNCTION
661 GOVAN
662 ST. ENOCH
663 TERMINUS JUNCTION
664 BAILLIESTON
665 FALKIRK
666 BATHGATE
667 MORNINGSIDE
668 CRAIGENTINNY
669 HAYMARKET
670 MORNINGSIDE
671 PAISLEY ST JAMES
672 LANGBANK
673 LARGS
674 AYR
675 PRESTWICK
676 AULDGIRTH
677 RICCARTON JUNCTION

#643 Resplendent in cleaned-up BR green livery, Cravens 2 car DMU waits in the goods yard at Turriff, the freight only terminus of the former GNSR line to Macduff, with the Branch Line Society railtour on 5th June 1965. A rake of freight wagons can be seen in the siding on the right, and the unusual combination of a pair of loading gauges can be seen on the left. *Roy Hamilton*

1Z

PREVIOUS PAGE:

#644 The same Cravens 2 car DMU as noted in the previous illustration, is seen at the platform and former station building of Oldmeldrum with the Branch Line Society railtour on 5th June 1965. *G.N. Turnbull*

#645 BRCW Type 2 Bo-Bo D.E. #D5307 approaches the closed station of Peterhead with the Peterhead Farewell Excursion railtour special on 5th September 1970, by which time the goods yard had been cleared of all wagons. *Mike Stephen*

#646 BR Type 4 1Co-Co1 D.E. #D10 Tryfan is seen in what maybe the only visit of one of the ten original Peak class locos to Aberdeen Ferryhill shed on 22nd June 1960. *Ken Nuttall*

#647 Andrew Barclay 0-4-0 205 h.p. D.M. shunter #D2420 trundles a well patronised brake van special along the intricate trackwork of the cobble inlayed railway network of Aberdeen Docks in November 1967. *Norris Forrest/TTT*

#648 Metro-Cammell 3-car DMU in rail blue livery at Mallaig with a special railtour in the summer of 1968. *Alan Carlaw*

#649 Unidentified NBL Type 2 Bo-Bo D.E. waits 'wrong line' at Tyndrum Lower with an engineers train on 23rd March 1966, as a lady and child 'scoot' over the station barrow crossing. *Jack Kernahan*

#650 NBL Type 2 Bo-Bo D.E. #D6118 and #D6123 at Crianlarich with the Eastfield brakedown crane in June 1969, when the mist shrouded Strath Fillan prevents discernable appreciation of the hills of Breadalbane beyond. *Alan Carlaw*

#651 D. Wickham 4-wheel diesel railbus #SC79968 decants passengers from a Glasgow University Railtour at the freight only terminus of Methven during May 1961. *Roy M.B. Crombie/SRPS*

#652 A very busy scene at Crieff on 11th October 1958 with A.C. Cars 4-wheel diesel railbus #SC79979 on a service from Comrie to Gleneagles sharing the station with ex-C.R. 4-2-2 #123 on a SLS railtour from Perth. In the distance an unidentified ex-LMS 4-6-0 Class 5 prepares to leave with a trip goods working to Perth yard via the Almond Valley Line.
WAC Smith/TTT

#653 BRCW Type 2 Bo-Bo D.E. #D5339 at Kirriemuir goods only station with the SLS/BLS 'Scottish Rambler' railtour on 23rd April 1962. The fact that there are so few enthusiasts in this composition is due to the patience of the accomplished photographer.
WAC Smith/TTT

#654 BR Type 2 Bo-Bo D.E. #D5122 at the former ornate station of St. Andrews with a Sunday Special service conveying passengers for an Alcan golf outing on 8th October 1967. Note the tablet catcher still in situ on the side of the locomotive beneath the near side cab window, which was quite unusual by this time. *Hamish Stevenson*

#655 Under the watchful guidance of the driver, passengers from a special BR service to mark the last day of operation on the steam operated swing bridge over the River Forth between Throsk and Alloa, walk towards the control tower on the middle of the bridge on 27th January 1968. Note the basic steps without a handrail allowing access to the passenger door of Park Royal 4-wheel diesel railbus #M79971. *Robin Nelson*

#656 Royal Mail trains invariably ran overnight throughout the former BR Scottish Region, therefore seeing such a train during daytime was a rarity. BRCW Type 2 Bo-Bo D.E. #D5329 waits at Stirling with a southbound service in June 1965. *Sandy Murdoch/TTT*

PREVIOUS PAGE:
#657 NBL Type 2 Bo-Bo D.E. #6121 (now bereft of its D prefix but still sporting its diamond shaped builders plate!) is seen at Denny with the Teuchtar Smith Special railtour, commemorating the total closure of the branch on 4th September 1971.
W.S. Sellar

#658 Gloucester R.C. & W. Co. 2-car DMU glides along the freight only Torrance branch (which used to run through to Kilsyth), with a driver training working from Maryhill Park on 25th February 1958. *WAC Smith/TTT*

#659 Looking in ex-works condition and attracting the attention of a railway worker, "Toffee Apple", Brush Type 2 AIA-AIA D.E. #D5511 runs past Cowlairs with an eastbound passenger service from Glasgow Queen Street on 9th July 1958.
Robin Nelson

#660 BR Derby 2-car lightweight DMU passes Shields Junction with a stopping service from Glasgow St. Enoch to Carlisle on the 18th May 1966. This was an unusual working by a LMR type of DMU on the Scottish Region. Note the erection of masts and steelwork to support the catenery for the impending electrification to Gourock and Wemyss Bay.
Robin Nelson

#661 The resident BR 0-6-0 350 h.p. D.E. shunter is obscured by the 4-wheel electric tram loco belonging to the nearby Fairfield Shipbuilding & Eng. Coy. Ltd., as it prepares to haul a short rake of two bogie bolster wagons along Govan Road from Govan Goods Yard with a special working for Glasgow tram and train enthusiasts on 2nd June 1962. Note the rakes of different types of goods wagons in the sidings, carrying mainly steel plates, sections, pipes and cable drums for the then busy Govan shipbuilding and ship repair yards. *WAC Smith/TTT*

#662 Performing a sad act of finality, EE Type 1 Bo-Bo DE. #D8117 propels the last rakes of empty coaching stock out of the now closed terminus of Glasgow St. Enoch on 25th June 1966. *Hamish Stevenson*

#663 EE Type 5 Co-Co D.E. #D9010 "The Kings Own Scottish Borderer" passes Terminus Junction, Glasgow with a special working on 8th May 1965. *Jack Kernahan*

#664 Metro-Vic Type 2 Co-Bo D.E. #D5704 has failed and broken down at Baillieston station whilst working a Clydesmill Power Station to Oakley N.C.B. sidings coal empty return working on 9th April 1960. *Roy Hamilton*

#665 EE Type 4 1Co-Co1 D.E. #40075 hauls a single westbound blue and grey liveried Royal Mail van over Falkirk Swing bridge on April 28th 1980. *Tom H. Noble*

#666 BR Pacer #143.006 east of Bathgate on 17th March 1986 with an Edinburgh – Bathgate – Edinburgh special service for press, councillors and officials of all of the bodies involved in the re-opening of the line. Pacers inaugurated the revenue earning service for a few weeks before Metro-Cammell Class 101 DMUs took over. *Tom H. Noble*

#667 Looking resplendent in ex-works condition, NBL Type 1 Bo-Bo D.E. #D8403 passes Morningside on 18th July 1958 en route to the Eastern Region of B.R., where it would be based for all of its brief and troublesome working life. *W.S. Sellar*

#668 Prototype Deltic EE Type 5 Co-Co D.E. at Craigentinny undergoing extensive builders trials on 12th June 1959. *Ken Falconer*

#669 Former BTH Type 1 Bo-Bo D.E. now re-numbered as DB 968001 performs the duty of an electric train heating unit at Haymarket on 14th August 1971. *Ken Falconer*

#670 Brush Type 2 AIA-AIA D.E. #D5511 still in ex-works condition passes through Morningside on the Edinburgh suburban circle with a lengthy transfer freight to Millerhill Yard on 18th July 1958. *W.S. Sellar*

#671 A brand new 3-car DMU built at the nearby Pressed Steel Co. Ltd., Linwood plant (on the truncated former Gleniffer Branch) is slowly driven by the builder's technicians resplendent in period style white boilersuits onto the Paisley-Gourock Line at Paisley St. James Junction prior to delivery to the BR Western Region during March 1960. *WAC Smith/TTT*

#672 Clayton Type 1 Bo-Bo D.E. #D8521 clatters through Langbank station with an engineers ballast train working on 29th May 1963, prior to the revelation of the locomotives chronic unreliability, which would soon result in their double-heading on almost every working on the Scottish Region. *Ken Nuttall*

#673 Unusual motive power in the form of EE Type 4 1Co-Co1 D.E. #D392 storms past Fairlie High signal box, adjàcent to the rail siding built for the conveyance of nuclear flasks to and from the nearby Hunterston A & B nuclear power stations, with a railtour special returning from Largs to Saltburn, Cleveland, on the Eastern region on 5th July 1963. *WAC Smith/TTT*

#674 BRCW Type 2 Bo-Bo D.E. #D5355 prepares to haul ex-LMS 4-6-2 Duchess #6233 "Duchess of Sutherland" from Ayr M.P.D. to Thetford, Eastern Region (for Bressingham Steam Museum) on 1st March 1971. *Derek Cross*

#675 Gloucester R.C. & W. Co. diesel railcar #SC 55013 passes the solum of the former branch to Glenburn Colliery, Prestwick with a management special working in November 1987. Note the outline of the island of Arran beyond. *Geo. C. O'Hara*

#676 Metro-Vic Type 2 Co-Bo #D5709 and #D5706 double head the 5.30 p.m. Glasgow St. Enoch to Carlisle stopping service near Auldgirth on the Nith Valley Route on 13th June 1959. This service was probably a filling-in run for these locomotives at that time, as they regularly hauled the Condor vacuum braked overnight container service between Glasgow Gushetfaulds and London Hendon, until their unreliability relegated them to the Furness line of the LMR.

TTT collection

#677 Unidentified Clayton Type 1 Bo-Bo D.E. leaves the open expanse of Riccarton Junction station with an engineers inspection train working between Carlisle and Edinburgh on the former Waverley Route during August 1966.

Roy M.B. Crombie/SRPS

Section 12

Dismantling

The 1963 report by Dr. Richard Beeching titled "The reshaping of British Railways" set in train the most thorough analysis of the credo of British Railways. Initiated under the Conservative administration of Harold MacMillan, most of the subsequent enactment of the report's recommendations was implemented without demur by the replacement Labour administration of Harold Wilson between 1964 and 1970.

The established route mileage inherited by the Scottish Region of B.R., and the many towns once rail connected were reduced considerably with a near decade long year on year notification of the "Withdrawal of railway passenger and goods services". Despite this country wide contraction, Scotland did retain a reduced passenger and goods carrying railway network up until the end of British Railways, but myopic closures of most branch lines and contentious circuitous parallel routes left the country with a much reduced "spoke" and "rim" railway network.

The speed with which the Scottish Region of B.R. set about the dismantling of lines closed under the Beeching diktat varied with incredible inconsistency throughout the country. Isolation of signalling and consolidation of track at affected junctions were implemented within hours of the last trains being in service. Whether a residual 'freight only' facility was to be retained thereafter dictated the initial scope of track demolition.

Recovery of track, metals, cabling and any sundry valuables was undertaken by a combination of contractors utilising demolition trains provided by B.R. The wilful destruction of several station buildings, signal boxes, goods and engine sheds along with bridges and other structures were the tangible consequences of line closures. The spread of photographs in this section depict several illustrations of B.R. locos and rolling stock assisting demolition contractors with the dismantling of seven former railway routes in Scotland.

LIST OF LOCATIONS ILLUSTRATED

678 KEMNAY
679 ABOYNE
680 ABOYNE
681 DESS
682 BALQUHIDDER
683 KINGSHOUSE
684 STRATHYRE
685 STRATHYRE
686 CRAIL
687 UDDINGSTON
688 HAPPENDON
689 COLDSTREAM
690 HAWICK
691 WAVERLEY ROUTE
692 MAXWELLTOWN
693 CREETOWN
694 LITTLE WATER OF FLEET VIADUCT
695 KILLYWHAN
696 CASTLE DOUGLAS
697 SHETTLESTON

#678 NBL Type 2 Bo-Bo D.E. #D6115 is seen in charge of a demolition and track recovery train near Kemnay on the former GNSR Alford branch on 27th September 1966. No evidence of mechanical lifting appliances can be seen, only a very labour intensive crew of gangers and their supervision. *W.S. Sellar*

#679 The former ornate GNSR station at Aboyne is in the early throes of sanctioned vandalism, as the demolition contractor prepares to dismantle the station, and recover the track during November 1969, utilising an elderly industrial diesel mechanical shunter built by the Hunslet Engine Company of Leeds. *Norris Forrest/TTT*

#680 The boarded-up signal box at Aboyne awaits the same fate as all others on the former Deeside Line as the demolition contractor moves east towards Aberdeen during November 1969.
Norris Forrest/TTT

#681 The same Deeside Line demolition train seen near Dess as track recovery continues during November 1969. The crawler crane lifts panels of redundant trackwork and places them on the flat wagons, which are then hauled back to an interim base where they are inspected for possible re-use or scrapping.
Norris Forrest/TTT

#682 NBL Type 2 Bo-Bo D.E. #D6119, spent part of its working life in revenue earning (if somewhat unreliable) service on the former Callander & Oban Line. After the line's closure in 1965 it is seen at Balquhidder displaying that 'forlorn face' which so symbolised the class, and its Western Region D.H. sisters. Panels of recovered track and the untidy detritus of dismantling operations can be seen strewn in the former yard. *Norris Forrest/TTT*

#683 The same locomotive as seen above is viewed ambling south between Kingshouse and Strathyre during the sad operation of dismantling the former Callander & Oban Line. *Norris Forrest/TTT*

#684 NBL Type 2 Bo-Bo D.E. #D6119 rolls into the former station at Strathyre during a demolition shuttle while assisting the contractor to dismantle and recover the trackwork and artefacts of the Callander and Oban Line. *Norris Forrest/TTT*

#685 NBL Type 2 Bo-BO D.E. #D6119 with dirty windows resembling a pair of eyes, rolls past the seemingly deserted village of Strathyre with a demolition train from the direction of Balquhidder whilst assisting track recovery of the Callander & Oban Line during 1966. *Norris Forrest/TTT*

#686 BR 0-6-0 350 h.p. D.E. Shunter #D3340 looks like it is in charge of a demolition train at the former NB station at Crail on 4th April 1967. *Hamish Stevenson*

#687 BR 0-6-0 350 h.p. D.E. shunter #D3209 is seen in charge of a demolition contractors train on the former NB line at Uddingston during June 1961.
Roy M.B. Crombie/SRPS

#688 A Ruston and Hornsby 48h.p. 4-wheel diesel mechanical industrial 0-4-0 shunter is seen at Happendon assisting with the dismantling and recovery of the former line from Lanark to Muirkirk during 1966.
Norris Forrest/TTT

#689 BR 0-6-0 350 h.p. D.E. shunter #D3729 marshalls four fitted 13-ton highfit open wagons during the dismantling of Coldstream station and the recovery of track and artefacts on 18th April 1970.
G.N. Turnbull

#690 The former NB goods yard at Hawick has been commandeered by the contractor dismantling and recovering track from the Waverley Route on 4th April 1971, as an unidentified BR 0-6-0 350 h.p. D.E. shunter prepares a rake of bogie bolster and conflat wagons to be loaded with materials from the operation. *Ken Falconer*

#691 Unidentified BR 0-6-0 350 h.p. D.E. shunter and a pair of bogie well wagons assist the demolition contractor somewhere on the former Waverley Route during March 1971. *G.N.Turnbull*

#692 BRCW Type 2 Bo-Bo D.E. #D5367 is seen in charge of a demolition train recovering track from Lochanhead on Longwood Bank, west of Maxwelltown on the former LMSR Dumfries-Stranraer Line during June 1968. *Norris Forrest/TTT*

#693 BR Type 2 Bo-Bo D.E. #D7620 in charge of a mixed rake of bogie bolster, plate and open wagons at Creetown during dismantling of the Dumfries-Stranraer Line on 17th May 1968. *Derek Cross*

#694 The crew of BRCW Type 2 Bo-Bo D.E. #5407 are smiling for the cameraman, but are not too pleased to be digging their own grave assisting the dismantling of the Dumfries-Stranraer Line at the Little Water of Fleet Viaduct near Gatehouse of Fleet on 12th August 1968. Note the cant of the track as the locomotive seems to be leaning towards the cameraman. *Derek Cross*

#695 BRCW Type 2 Bo-Bo D.E. #D5353 passes through Killywhan light engine en route to pick-up a demolition train near Dalbeattie on the removal and recovery of the former Dumfries-Stranraer Line on 16th May 1968.

Jack Kernahan

#696 BRCW Type 2 Bo-Bo DE. #D5353 and a brace of different brake vans seen near Castle Douglas assisting the demolition contractor on the dismantling of the Dumfries-Stranraer Line during May 1968. *Jack Kernahan*

#697 At least half a dozen of the NBL Type 2 Bo-Bo D.E. #D61XX class (with D6151 nearest the camera) are seen awaiting the cutters torch at the J. McWilliam Scrapyard, Shettleston in 1972, a year after the withdrawal of the last operating member of the class. Built in the late 1950's at the nearby Springburn Works of the world famous North British Locomotive Co. Ltd., this class of nearly sixty diesel electric locomotives was not a success. They did however work on many lines within the former BR Scottish Region during their short lives. They had a stylish bodyshell with a pair of parallel convex windows above a slightly bulbous corridor connection door. These combined features gave the locomotives a somewhat sombre looking "face". *WAC Smith/TTT*

INDEX

LOCATION	TYPE OF DIESEL TRACTION (Abbvd)	PHOTO No.
Dalwhinnie	EE Type 3 Co-Co #37260 "Radio Highland"	392
Dalmarnock	Metro-Cammell 4-car hybrid DMU	558
Dalmarnock (London Road)	EE Type I Bo-Bo #D8121	609
Darvel	Unidentified Park Royal 4-wheel railbus	39
Dava	Unidentified BRCW Type 2 Bo-Bo	239
Dava	BR Type 2 Bo-Bo #D5123	385
Dava Summit	BR Type 2 Bo-Bo #D5128	146
Dawsholm loco shed	Unidentified BR 0-6-0 Shunter	24
Denny	NBL Type 2 Bo-Bo #6121 (minus 'D' prefix)	657
Dess	Hunslet Industrial Shunter	681
Dingwall	EE Type I Bo-Bo #D8032	233
Dingwall	BRCW Type 2 Bo-Bo #26039	382
Dollar	Park Royal 4-wheel railbus #SC79972	64
Dollar	Unidentified D. Wickham 4-wheel railbus	65
Doune	Hybrid Metro-Cammell 2-car DMU & Cravens 2-car DMU	285
Drem	Metro-Cammell & Gloucester R.C. & W. Co. 2-car DMU	90
Drem Junction	Gloucester R.C. & W. Co. 4-car DMU	91
Drongan	BR Type 2 Bo-Bo #25244 & EE Type I Bo-Bo #20089	466
Drymen (Croftamie)	BR 0-6-0 Shunter #D3534	602
Duddingston	Gloucester R.C. & W. Co. 2-car DMU	92
Dufftown	EE Type 4 ICo-CoI #40168	575
Dumbarton	BRCW Type 2 Bo-Bo #27020	185
Dumbarton	BRCW Type 2 Bo-Bo #27009	439
Dumbarton East	Unidentified BRCW Type 2 Bo-Bo	186
Dumfries	BR Type 2 Bo-Bo #25230	570
Dumfries	BRCW Type 2 Bo-Bo #26029	639
Duncraig	Unidentified BRCW Type 2 Bo-Bo	484
Dundee	Clayton Type I Bo-Bo #D8618	408
Dundee	A. Barclay 0-4-0 Shunter #D2415	584
Dundee Tay Bridge	BRCW Type 2 Bo-Bo's #D5305 & #D5306	271
Dundee Tay Bridge loco shed	Various NBL 0-4-0 Shunters	13
Dunkeld & Birnham	Unidentified BRCW Type 2 Bo-Bo	258
Dunphail	Unidentified BRCW Type 2 Bo-Bo	240
Dunphail	BR Type 2 Bo-Bo #D5123	386
Dunphail	Unidentified BR Type 2 Bo-Bo	387
Dunragit	BR Type 4 ICo-CoI #D24	326
Dyce	Unidentified EE Type 4 ICo-CoI & BR Type 2 Bo-Bo	398
Dyce	BR Swindon 3-car DMU & Gloucester R.C. & W. Co. single railcar	492
Dyce Junction	BR Swindon 3-car DMU & Glouceser RC. & W. Co. railcar	332
East Kilbride	BR Derby 3-car DMU	109
East Kilbride	EE Type I Bo-Bo #20108	565
East Kilbride	Unidentified Clayton Type I Bo-Bo	608
Eastfield loco shed	Unidentified BRCW Type 2 Bo-Bo	22
Edinburgh Princes St.	Unidentified Clayton Type I Bo-Bo	317
Edinburgh Waverley	BR Swindon 6-car DMU	93
Edinburgh Waverley	EE Type 5 Co-Co #D9000 "Royal Scots Grey"	175
Edinburgh Waverley	Brush Type 5 Co-Co #D47709 "The Lord Provost" and other locos	318
Edinburgh Waverley	EE Type 5 Co-Co #D9014 "The Duke of Wellington's Regt."	319
Elgin	Unidentified NBL Type 2 Bo-Bo	149
Elgin	NBL Type 2 Bo-Bo #D6143	243
Elgin	Various unidentified BRCW Type 2 Bo-Bo's	244
Elgin	BR Type 2 Bo-Bo #25227	513
Elgin loco shed	A. Barclay 0-4-0 Shunter #D2414	11
Enterkine Viaduct	BRCW Type 2 Bo-Bo #27042 & BR Type 2 #25072	465
Fairlie	EE Type 4 ICo-CoI #D392	673
Falahill Bank	Unidentified BRCW Type 2 Bo-Bo	226
Falkirk	Park Royal 4-wheel railbus #M79971	55
Falkirk	BR Swindon 6-car DMU	99
Falkirk	EE Type 4 ICo-CoI #40075	665
Falkland Yard	EE Type 4 ICo-CoI #40022	567
Fauldhouse	Gloucester R.C. & W. Co. 4-car DMU	96
Fauldhouse	BR Swindon 6-car DMU	97
Fearn	BRCW Type 2 Bo-Bo's #26039 & #26045	480
Ferryhill loco shed	Unidentified Type I Bo-Bo; Type 2 Bo-Bo; Type 4 Co-Co	8
Ferryhill loco shed	EE Type 5 Co-Co #55015 "Tulyar"	9
Ferryhill loco shed	BR Type 4 ICo-CoI #D10 "Tryfan"	646
Finnart	Unidentified Park Royal 4-wheel railbus	41
Fisherrow Junction	Metro-Cammell 2-car DMU	346
Forfar	NBL Type 2 Bo-Bo #D6145	163
Forfar	EE Type 4 ICo-CoI #D361	164
Forfar	NBL Type 2 Bo-Bo #D6106	254
Forfar	BRCW Type 2 Bo-Bo #27208	534
Forres	BR Swindon 6-car DMU	67
Forres	BRCW Type 2 Bo-Bo #D5331	238
Forres loco shed	BR 0-6-0 Shunter #D3735	4
Fort William	BRCW Type 2 Bo-Bo #D5365	264
Fort William	Unidentified BR Type 2 Bo-Bo	538
Forth Bridge	Gloucester R.C. & W. Co. 2-car DMU	89
Fouldubs	BR 0-6-0 Shunter #08505	596
Fountainhall	Metro-Cammell 3-car DMU	138
Fraserburgh	Cravens 2-car DMU & Metro-Cammell 2-car DMU & NBL Type 2 Bo-Bo #D6145	74
Fraserburgh	NBL Type 2 Bo-Bo #D6141	157
Fraserburgh	BRCW Type 2 Bo-Bo #D5347	250
Fraserburgh	Unidentified NBL Type 2 Bo-Bo	401
Fraserburgh	Cravens 2-car DMU & 2 Unidentified NBL Type 2 Bo-Bos	514
Fraserburgh	Unidentified NBL Type 2 Bo-Bo	515
Fraserburgh	BR Type 2 Bo-Bo #25023	516
Fraserburgh	BRCW Type 2 Bo-Bo #26029	517
Fraserburgh loco shed	Unidentified NBL Type 2 Bo-Bo	6
Fraserburgh loco shed	BRCW Type 2 Bo-Bo #D5315	7
Fullwood Junction	NBL Type 2 Bo-Bo #D6115	349
Galashiels	Unidentified BR Type 4 ICo-CoI	325
Garelochhead	BRCW Type 2 Bo-Bo #D5348	184
Garelochhead	BRCW Type 2 Bo-Bo #D5363	437
Gartly	BRCW Type 2 Bo-Bo's #26040 & #26041	490
Garve	Unidentified BRCW Type 2 Bo-Bo	144

BACK COVER PICTURES

Top Picture:
Unidentified BRCW Type 2 Bo-Bo D.E. at Ballachulish with a service for Connel Ferry in May 1964. Note the "Pap of Glencoe" beyond the slate quarry. *G.N. Turnbull*

Middle Picture:
BRCW Type 2 Bo-Bo #D5366 pauses at Fort William station prior to heading a mixed train to Mallaig containing two Blue Spot insul fish vans on 9th October 1964.
John M. Boyes – The Armstrong Railway Photographic Trust

Bottom Picture:
A pair of unidentified BRCW Type 2 Bo-Bo D.E.'s power up Glenogle with a service from Glasgow Buchanan Street to Oban on 8th August, 1965. *G.N. Turnbull*

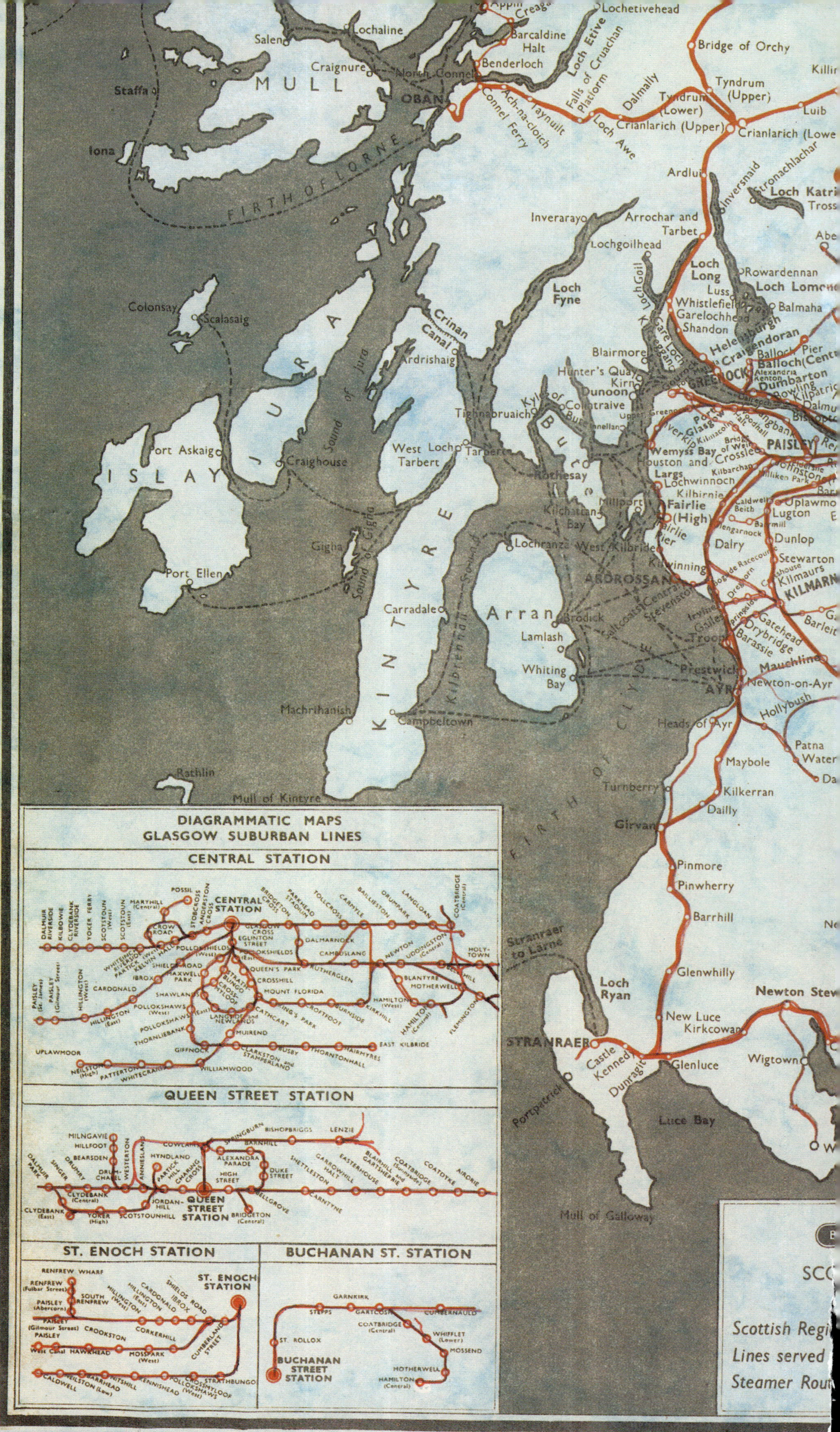
MULL
Staffa
Iona
Salen
Lochaline
Craignure
Oban
Appin
Creagan
Barcaldine Halt
Benderloch
North Connel
Connel Ferry
Ach-na-cloich
Taynuilt
Loch Etive
Falls of Cruachan Platform
Loch Awe
Dalmally
Lochetivehead
Bridge of Orchy
Tyndrum (Upper)
Tyndrum (Lower)
Crianlarich (Upper)
Crianlarich (Lower)
Luib
FIRTH OF LORNE
Colonsay
Scalasaig
JURA
Sound of Jura
ISLAY
Port Askaig
Craighouse
Port Ellen
Gigha
Sound of Gigha
Inveraray
Arrochar and Tarbet
Ardlui
Inversnaid
Stronachlachar
Loch Katrine
Lochgoilhead
Loch Long
Loch Fyne
Loch Goil
Rowardennan
Loch Lomond
Luss
Balmaha
Whistlefield
Garelochhead
Shandon
Helensburgh
Craigendoran
Crinan Canal
Ardrishaig
Blairmore
Hunter's Quay
Kirn
Dunoon
Colintraive
Tighnabruaich
Kyles of Bute
Bute
Rothesay
West Loch Tarbert
Tarbert
Wemyss Bay
Largs
Fairlie (High)
Kilchattan Bay
Millport
KINTYRE
Carradale
Lochranza
West Kilbride
Ardrossan
Arran
Brodick
Lamlash
Whiting Bay
Kilbrannan Sound
Machrihanish
Campbeltown
Mull of Kintyre
Rathlin
Dalry
Kilwinning
Kilmarnock
Irvine
Troon
Prestwick
AYR
Newton-on-Ayr
Mauchline
Heads of Ayr
Hollybush
Maybole
Patna
Kilkerran
Dailly
Turnberry
Girvan
FIRTH OF CLYDE
Pinmore
Pinwherry
Barrhill
Glenwhilly
New Luce
Kirkcowan
Newton Stewart
Wigtown
Loch Ryan
Stranraer
Stranraer to Larne
Castle Kennedy
Dunragit
Glenluce
Portpatrick
Luce Bay
Mull of Galloway
Paisley
Greenock
Dumbarton
Lugton
Dunlop
Stewarton
Uplawmoor
DIAGRAMMATIC MAPS
GLASGOW SUBURBAN LINES
CENTRAL STATION
QUEEN STREET STATION
ST. ENOCH STATION
BUCHANAN ST. STATION
Scottish Region
Lines served
Steamer Routes